The Evidence fo
Psychodynamic
Psychotherapy

This book delivers a concise yet comprehensive introduction to the evidence for psychodynamic psychotherapy through explanations of research organized around therapy processes relevant to practicing clinicians and informed researchers.

Each chapter presents an event within dynamic therapy, from interpretation to termination, along with a narrative to help readers understand the why and the how of the process. Written in accessible and engaging language, each short chapter is a synthesis of findings in each topic area, going beyond subjects interesting only to researchers to aspects of practice relevant to therapists of all schools of thought.

The Evidence for Psychodynamic Psychotherapy is written for therapists to pick up and put down between clients, for mental health researchers to quickly find support for a point they wish to make, and for educators to assign brief readings to bolster students' confidence in dynamic therapy.

Kevin McCarthy is Associate Professor in the Department of Professional Psychology at Chestnut Hill College, Clinical Associate Professor of Psychology in Psychiatry, and Director of the Residency Psychotherapy Curriculum in the Department of Psychiatry at the University of Pennsylvania, USA.

Carla Capone is a clinical psychology PsyD student at Chestnut Hill College, Philadelphia, USA.

Liat Leibovich, PhD, is a clinical psychologist and licensed supervisor in psychotherapy and psychodiagnosis working at "Ahava" children's home, in private practice, and as a lecturer in "Mifrasim" Institute and Haifa University, Israel.

Routledge Introductions to Contemporary Psychoanalysis

Aner Govrin, Ph.D.
Series Editor

Yael Peri Herzovich, Ph.D.
Executive Editor

Tair Caspi, Ph.D.
Executive Editor

"Routledge Introductions to Contemporary Psychoanalysis" is one of the prominent psychoanalytic publishing ventures of our day.

The series' aim is to become an encyclopedic enterprise of psychoanalysis, with each entry given its own book.

This comprehensive series is designed to illuminate the intricate landscape of psychoanalytic theory and practice. In this collection of concise yet illuminating volumes, we delve into the influential figures, groundbreaking concepts, and transformative theories that shape the contemporary psychoanalytic landscape.

At the heart of each volume lies a commitment to clarity, accessibility, and depth. Our expert authors, renowned scholars and practitioners in their respective fields guide readers through the complexities of psychoanalytic thought with precision and enthusiasm. Whether you are a seasoned psychoanalyst, a student eager to explore the field, or a curious reader seeking insight into the human psyche, our series offers a wealth of knowledge and insight.

Each volume serves as a gateway into a specific aspect of psychoanalytic theory and practice. From the pioneering works of Sigmund Freud to the innovative contributions of modern theorists such as Antonino Ferro and Michal Eigen, our series covers a diverse range of topics, including seminal figures, key concepts, and emerging trends. Whether you are interested in classical psychoanalysis, object relations theory, or the intersection of neuroscience and psychoanalysis, you will find a wealth of resources within our collection.

One of the hallmarks of our series is its interdisciplinary approach. While rooted in psychoanalytic theory, our volumes draw upon insights from psychology, philosophy, sociology, and other disciplines to offer a holistic understanding of the human mind and its complexities.

Each volume in the series is crafted with the reader in mind, balancing scholarly rigor with engaging prose. Whether you are embarking on your journey into psychoanalysis or seeking to deepen your understanding of specific topics, our series provides a clear and comprehensive roadmap.

Moreover, our series is committed to fostering dialogue and debate within the psychoanalytic community. Each volume invites readers to critically engage with the material, encouraging reflection, discussion, and further exploration.

We invite you to join us on this journey of discovery as we explore the ever-evolving landscape of psychoanalysis.

ראש הטופס
Aner Govrin—Editor

The Evidence for Psychodynamic Psychotherapy

A Contemporary Introduction

Kevin McCarthy,
Carla Capone, and
Liat Leibovich

Routledge
Taylor & Francis Group

LONDON AND NEW YORK

Designed cover image: © Michal Heiman, Asylum 1855–2020, *The Sleeper* (video, psychoanalytic sofa and Plate 34), exhibition view, Herzliya Museum of Contemporary Art, 2017

First published 2025
by Routledge
4 Park Square, Milton Park, Abingdon, Oxon OX14 4RN

and by Routledge
605 Third Avenue, New York, NY 10158

Routledge is an imprint of the Taylor & Francis Group, an informa business

© 2025 Kevin McCarthy, Carla Capone, and Liat Leibovich

The right of Kevin McCarthy, Carla Capone, and Liat Leibovich to be identified as authors of this work has been asserted in accordance with sections 77 and 78 of the Copyright, Designs and Patents Act 1988.

British Library Cataloguing-in-Publication Data
A catalogue record for this book is available from the British Library

ISBN: 978-1-032-34642-7 (hbk)
ISBN: 978-1-032-34641-0 (pbk)
ISBN: 978-1-003-32316-7 (ebk)

DOI: 10.4324/9781003323167

Typeset in Times New Roman
by KnowledgeWorks Global Ltd.

To my father, who always wanted reprints of my publications to highlight and write on. Every time I spoke with him, he would ask how this book was coming. Dad, you know I would give you a thousand copies if I still could.

Kevin McCarthy

Forever grateful to the mentors who have guided, inspired, and put their trust in me throughout my graduate training, my lovely friends who never hear the end of interesting psychological research findings, my eternally supportive family, and my wonderful partner whose warmth, intellect, and curiosity both as a clinician and overall human being I aspire to always.

Carla Capone

I would like to dedicate this book to my loving and supportive family. Combining the worlds of clinical practice and research would not have been possible without your help: my parents, Shoshi and Yochanan; my children, Ido, Noga, and Amir; and my partner, Gabi.

Liat Leibovich

Contents

Introduction

> *It is the intention to provide a scientific psychology, that is, to propose psychological processes as certain, quantifiable states of observable material things, thereby making them clear and incontrovertible.*
>
> (Freud, 1895, p. 387)

In his earliest writings, Freud attempted to understand what was transmitted across neurons in the brain. His solution was a quotient of dynamic energy with hydraulic properties that could be measured and conserved and that brought about symptom experiences when overexcited. As he turned his inquiry from brain and body toward the mind and relationships, Freud retained this model both in his theory of drives and in the anticipation of orderly, discoverable processes underlying mental life (Gundersen, 2022). Psychoanalysis, then, was conceived as a research methodology as well as a treatment modality (Fonagy, 2003; Pine, 2006). Psychodynamic therapy (PDT) emerged from this nexus with the expectation of continuing empirical research and discovery. So what is this evidence, and where might it be found? How can we get it to practitioners and researchers who can convert it to the benefit of clients and the public?

The purpose of this text is to present the extensive empirical research in support for PDT. Psychodynamic clinicians can use this evidence to confirm and enhance the treatments they provide to patients every day. Trainees can gain confidence that the PDT they are learning is effective. Therapists and researchers of other theoretical orientations can raise their awareness of dynamic processes that might be operating in their areas of expertise. We, the authors, are practitioners, trainees, and researchers ourselves. We hope to give a contextualization of the

DOI: 10.4324/9781003323167-1

research that we as therapists have found helpful in our own work with patients.

Approach to Approaching Data

I have examined your experimental studies for the verification of the psychoanalytic assertions with interest. I cannot put much value on these confirmations because the wealth of reliable observations on which these assertions rest make them independent of experimental verification. Still, it can do no harm.

(Freud, 1934, in Rozensweig, 1985, pp. 171–172)

As a scientist, Freud recognized that evidence and knowledge comes not just from empirical study. The clinical process, the depth of the therapy relationship, and a focus on experience produce data beyond what can be collected through an inferential approach (Rozensweig, 1985). This book will be unique in that it will start off thought with the assumption that what psychodynamic practitioners are currently doing in therapy is already best quality. PDT therapists will continue to help patients feel better and make changes in their lives, and empirical research can only improve on this good foundation. Further, we want to get the findings from empirical research to practitioners in ways that add value to what they already do and begin discussion of feedback on which parts of research are worthwhile, and which are missing the mark.

In this text, we will occasionally distinguish between clinical work and empirical research. However, we give the caveat now specifically that there is no ownership of science or scholarship. A therapist is as much engaged in research about their patients and the problems people encounter as a researcher is ultimately striving to help others through their study. One is not more noble than the other. Our intent is to introduce empirical research findings in PDT in a complement to what many readers already know and value, not to convince or colonize.

Structure of This Book

As good scientists should, we will lay out our method here. Each chapter reviews the empirical research for an aspect or process from PDT (e.g., expressive interventions, termination). We will use plain, transparent language in describing these phenomena, attempting to avoid both research and psychoanalytic jargon or shorthand. Chapters will be very brief (5–8 pages) in order to be readable in between the many time pressures that therapists, trainees, and researchers have. We have selectively picked references to be recent empirical reviews or important contributions that we believed our readers would find worthwhile. Many will be available on the internet or through the networking application researchgate.net.

We will concentrate on understanding *what* the research has said (the approach of most empirical reviews) and the *how* and *why* of the ways the research was conducted. Theory, definition, and measurement will receive heavy attention. A fundamental part of empirical research is *operationalization*, or making theoretical ideas measurable. Researchers have been creative trying to fit psychoanalytic concepts into realistic or tangible derivatives, but sometimes the decisions made in this process capture only part of—or even something totally different—than what clinicians see and work with in practice. Appraising this step is critical to evaluating the PDT literature and further refining it. We also spotlight measures commonly used in research that might be useful (and in many cases, free) to clinicians and other researchers.

We will then describe the findings around the construct. We will use the literature to portray how PDT and psychoanalytic concepts emerge in the process or in the person, in response to what, and how they are best worked with. We will use example studies so readers gain a sense of how the research was conducted. We will also highlight important or surprising results that promise intriguing areas for exploration. We round out each chapter with a section on innovations that epitomize the direction of research findings for practice (e.g., new treatment models) and offer avenues for future thought and study.

Overview of Chapters

Chapter 1 will first define PDT, psychoanalytic psychotherapy, and psychoanalysis and lay out the differences among them. We will describe the ways that PDT and treatments of other theoretical orientations have been measured and distinguished in research and present the data on the prevalence of PDT in practice and training across the world. Chapter 2 will review the philosophical assumptions by which we generally understand and apply psychoanalytic ideas. We will compare these ideas with the assumptions held by many empirical researchers, exploring the limitations and benefits that an empirical approach has for PDT. Chapter 3 presents summary data for the outcomes of PDT. We will see for which problems, disorders, and populations PDT improves patients' symptoms and functioning.

Next, we will examine the therapeutic relationship and its many components, something PDT practitioners will recognize as the essential means by which therapy runs. Chapter 4 reviews empirical research on transference, the interpersonal patterns patients bring to therapy that repeat in their relationships and relate to symptom experiences. Chapter 5 will explore countertransference, the feeling states therapists have in response to the process of PDT that can alter and inform the direction of the treatment. We explore the therapeutic alliance in Chapter 6, the part of the therapeutic relationship shared by client and therapist to facilitate the work of PDT. Alliance is the strongest predictor of therapy outcome in psychotherapy research and as a result has a rich elaboration in the empirical literature. One area taking central stage in research right now is alliance rupture and repair, reviewed in Chapter 7. Influenced by current relational and intersubjective psychoanalytic thought, mapping how ruptures are resolved is pragmatic for the process of PDT and a way of creating change through the therapy relationship. The real relationship, also out of the relational tradition, is the genuine connection by which the patient and therapist see one another as complex and imperfect human beings. Research on this refreshing topic is presented in Chapter 8.

PDT entails two types of interventions that therapists use with their clients. Supportive interventions help the patient actively solve conflict between their internal motivations and external demands and to also build alliance with their therapist. Perhaps overlooked in clinical and empirical literatures, we review research on the frequency and effects of supportive techniques in Chapter 9. Expressive interventions expose unconscious conflict and raise awareness of problems in the patient's functioning. Chapter 10 presents the research about these techniques and their nuanced associations with therapy process and patient improvement, including studies on how therapists competently deliver these techniques.

PDT follows a timeframe that loosely can be construed as socialization, working through, and termination. Chapter 11 covers socialization, the initial period in which patient and therapist learn about one another and establish the formulation. We will review research on preparing patients for PDT, identifying clients likely to benefit from PDT, accommodating patient preferences for treatment, and increasing hope and expectancy for change. Chapter 12 is on the working through, the middle phase of PDT in which patients' interpersonal patterns are re-examined to bring about clarity and commitment to change. We will investigate research on therapeutic "dose," or the amount of treatment needed for improvement, and typical profiles of patients' response to PDT. Termination is the ending of therapy and an important tool in PDT to consolidate change. In Chapter 13, we will explore the processes and experiences of ending in PDT, including factors related to dropout or premature termination. Time-limited PDT offers a specific length of therapy set at the outset of treatment. Having this boundary alters how patients and therapists work in therapy, and we will examine research findings and methodology for brief PDT in Chapter 14.

Mechanisms are factors that PDT changes within the person that ultimately lead to improvement. Investigating how these mechanisms operate gets into the therapeutic action of PDT. Research on the moderators and mediators of change can teach us ways that we can improve what we provide for patients, including how psychodynamic constructs occur in other treatments. Chapters 15 and 16 review studies of insight and psychological defenses, two of the earliest theoretical explanations for change in PDT. Chapter 17 looks at research on attachment, the object- or relationship-seeking drive in psychoanalysis that became the most widely researched topic in general psychology. Chapter 18 examines quality of object relations, the cognitive–affective maps and their structure that guide perception and behavior in relationships. Mentalization, or reflective functioning, is the developmental skill by which the person applies their object relations. This new area of research is displayed in Chapter 19. Finally, PDT alters brain functioning in observable ways that confirm theoretical propositions. Chapter 20 will review some of the neuroscience as applied to PDT.

Much of the research covered in this book and in psychotherapy research speaks for PDT with individual adults as traditionally practiced. Treatment for children and adolescents has almost an equally long tradition in PDT and has gained strong research backing in the last few years, reviewed in Chapter 21. PDT clinicians and investigators have also been more active considering how identity and cultural diversity influences the process and experience of PDT. Chapter 22 examines research showing how therapists and clients can come together and use their differences to facilitate greater connection and understanding of relationships.

References

Fonagy, P. (2003). Psychoanalysis today. *World Psychiatry*, *2*(2), 73.

Freud, S. (1895). Allgemeiner plan. *Gesammelte Werke*, *18*, 387–477.

Gundersen, S. (2022). Mechanisms and fundamental principles in Freudian explanations. *Scandinavian Psychoanalytic Review*, *45*(2), 87–95. https://doi.org/10.1080/01062301.2023.2274145

Pine, F. (2006). The psychoanalytic dictionary: A position paper on diversity and its unifiers. *Journal of the American Psychoanalytic Association*, *54*(2), 463–491.

Rozensweig, S. (Ed.). (1985). *A century of psychology as science*. American Psychological Association.

Part I

Foundations

Chapter 1

Distinguishing Psychodynamic Psychotherapy

Definitions

Psychodynamic therapy (PDT) is a depth-focused relational treatment that uses psychoanalytic principles to explore unconscious motivations and conflict. It has a focus or formulation individually created for each person that describes the nature of their problem and the interpersonal contexts in which it arises. Patients and therapists apply this pattern to current and past relational experiences to help the patient gain insight or emotional mastery over its occurrence (see Chapters 15–20 on mechanisms of action in PDT). The relationship between the client and therapist is paramount because those patterns are repeated there and can be closely inspected for their purpose and utility. The relationship is also where clients will find the support and encouragement they need to make changes in their life.

We should draw a distinction between PDT and psychoanalysis, the parent treatment method that gave PDT its theoretical foundations and procedures. Psychoanalysis, the larger focus of this series, is a theory, an inquiry method, and a treatment that is as variegated as the human experience it endeavors to explain (Fonagy, 2003; Pine, 2006). Psychoanalytic treatment entails multiple contacts between the patient and therapist weekly for the development of an intense emotional relationship that is examined for motivations, symptoms, and historical antecedents. A psychoanalysis is complete when all conflicts have been exposed and examined, including the experience of termination and separation, and may take many months or years. Table 1.1 depicts ways that PDT and psychoanalysis vary on several dimensions. Much of the empirical literature speaks to PDT because it is simpler and easier to model and requires fewer person and training resources compared to psychoanalysis.

DOI: 10.4324/9781003323167-3

Table 1.1 Dimensions of Psychodynamic Therapy and Psychoanalysis

Dimension	Psychodynamic Therapy	Psychoanalysis
Frequency	Once or twice weekly	3 or more sessions per week
Duration	Time-limited or open-ended Typically 3–12 months	Open-ended Typically 2 or more years
Client posture	Sitting up; face-to-face Encouraging interaction	Many times reclining Therapist not in view
Focus	Mostly outward focus Some attention inward	Encouraging inward focus
Goal	More specific aim or objective	Exploratory, non-directive
Interventions	More supportive (resolving conflict) Some expressive (uncovering conflict)	Mostly expressive (uncovering conflict)
Use of relationship	Support for change Examination of interpersonal patterns	Used as focus of treatment
Therapist stance	Alliance-building More active	Observant, watchful Facilitating expression of conflict

Measurement

PDT is a theoretical orientation from which therapists draw their specific stances, interventions, and procedures in their work with clients. To identify what system a therapist practices under, therapists can be asked what type of therapy that they generally perform with patients or that they provided in a particular session with a checklist of different orientations (e.g., client-centered or cognitive-behavioral therapy [CBT]). Other times, therapists rate on a scale how much they follow each of a number of orientations. They give separate scores for each of the modalities showing the degree to which they are influenced by that system. Psychoanalysis is often an option given on these lists, but researchers will frequently combine psychoanalysis and PDT when reporting these data. These methods do not account for certification or training (typically measured as years of experience) or for therapists' differences in definitions.

PDT is also measured by its component parts in a session. Researchers use tools assessing therapy behaviors like how many interpretations were given or how much the therapist and client focused on past experiences (see Chapter 10). Adherence and competence measures are specific instruments of how much therapists followed a specific PDT model or treatment manual and how well their work was done. Cutoff scores determine whether a therapist maintained compliance and are used in research trials to ensure a treatment was delivered as intended. Typically outside judges use these measures for sessions of PDT, but therapists and patients can also make these ratings.

Significance

PDT is regularly declared to be one of the most practiced treatments worldwide when therapists are surveyed about how they work. Psychodynamic thinking and practice has become part of many cultures, synonymous with psychotherapy itself and eradicating many disorders seen by early psychoanalysts (Yakushko, 2021). The largest international survey of over 10,000 therapists showed that a PDT orientation was the most strongly endorsed, with at least 62% of participants reporting at least some PDT element to their practice (Orlinsky et al., 2020). Globally, 49% of therapist training programs required some competency in PDT (Orlinsky et al., 2024). Psychotherapists who practice in other modalities are likely to choose PDT for their own personal therapy (Orlinsky et al., 2011). Despite concerns that the field may be in decline (Yakushko, 2021), estimates of professionals endorsing a PDT or psychoanalytic orientation have remained relatively stable in the past few decades (Norcross et al., 2023). In some areas of the world, PDT is the fastest growing form of therapeutic intervention (Yao et al., 2023).

PDT can readily be distinguished from other types of therapies in its process and interventions. From observer, therapist, and client rating perspectives, PDT therapists employ more PDT interventions and less alternative techniques in sessions than do therapists of other orientations, and vice versa (see Chapter 10). To identify what actions made PDT unique from other therapy orientations in comparative psychotherapy process studies, Hilsenroth and colleagues (2005) reviewed studies using empirical measures of therapy process to contrast elements found in psychodynamic-interpersonal and CBT approaches. Table 1.2 depicts the themes that occurred across the findings that caused PDT and CBT to be distinct.

Table 1.2 Empirically Determined Differences between Psychodynamic-
Interpersonal and Cognitive-Behavioral Therapies

Psychodynamic-Interpersonal	Cognitive-Behavioral
Focusing on patients' affect and interpersonal experiences	Focusing on patients' cognition
Identifying defenses, avoidance, and treatment-interfering behaviors	Assigning homework
Finding patterns in relationships	Actively directing session activity
Attending to past experiences	Attending to future experiences
Examining the therapeutic relationship	Teaching specific coping skills
Exploring patients' wishes, dreams, or fantasies	Providing psychoeducation

Note: Adapted from Hilsenroth et al. (2005).

New Directions

When we look at the empirical research that is mainly on PDT, we will be missing much of the depth and the relationship that is explored in psychoanalysis. PDT and time-limited approaches must focus on goals that are achievable within the specified period of therapy, which will typically be symptom or problem reduction. There is less opportunity for exploration, development, and healing, making the content and process indescribably different between the two. Consequently, outcomes will also be different between PDT and psychoanalysis. Therapists will have different levels of training, as psychoanalysts are generally able to do PDT but not the reverse. Patients will devote different amounts of time, effort, and mental capacity to the treatment.

Our assessment of findings in the research literature is that processes and outcomes in PDT and psychoanalysis substantially overlap, as least as can be determined with empirical methods. PDT shares more similarity in its therapeutic action to psychoanalysis than do other psychological treatments like CBT and can be a model for many psychoanalytic processes. The activity level and the time limit of PDT jumpstart and bring to the surface many unconscious processes that otherwise would take longer to emerge. Symptom change and problem resolution certainly occur in psychoanalysis, and the patterns and sequelae are often similar when they occur as in PDT. While empirical research of psychoanalysis is possible but occurs less frequently because it is more challenging, we believe that PDT can be a reasonable stand-in to validate many aspects of psychoanalytic psychology and treatment.

References

Fonagy, P. (2003). Psychoanalysis today. *World Psychiatry, 2*(2), 73.

Hilsenroth, M. J., Blagys, M. D., Ackerman, S. J., Bonge, D. R., & Blais, M. A. (2005). Measuring psychodynamic-interpersonal and cognitive-behavioral techniques: Development of the comparative psychotherapy process scale. *Psychotherapy: Theory, Research, Practice, Training, 42*(3), 340–356. https://doi.org/10.1037/0033-3204.42.3.340

Norcross, J. C., Rocha, M. N., & Chrysler, A. A. (2023). Psychologists conducting psychotherapy in 2022: Contemporary practices and historical patterns of the society for the advancement of psychotherapy. *Psychotherapy, 60*(4), 587–592. https://doi.org/10.1037/pst0000493

Orlinsky, D. E., Messina, I., Hartmann, A., Willutzki, U., Heinonen, E., Rønnestad, M. H., & Schröder, T. (2024). Ninety psychotherapy training programmes across the globe: Variations and commonalities in an international context. *Counselling and Psychotherapy Research, 24*(2), 558–571.

Orlinsky, D. E., Rønnestad, M. H., Hartmann, A., Heinonen, E., & Willutzki, U. (2020). The personal self of psychotherapists: Dimensions, correlates, and relations with clients. *Journal of Clinical Psychology, 76*(3), 461–475. https://doi.org/10.1002/jclp.22678

Orlinsky, D. E., Schofield, M. J., Schroder, T., & Kazantzis, N. (2011). Utilization of personal therapy by psychotherapists: A practice-friendly review and a new study. *Journal of Clinical Psychology, 67*(8), 828–842.

Pine, F. (2006). The psychoanalytic dictionary: A position paper on diversity and its unifiers. *Journal of the American Psychoanalytic Association, 54*(2), 463–491.

Yakushko, O. (2021). The exclusion of psychoanalysis in academic and organized U.S. psychology: On voodooism, witch-hunts, and the legion of followers. *Psychoanalytic Inquiry, 41*(8), 638–653. https://doi.org/10.1080/07351690.2021.1983405

Yao, L., Wang, Z., Gu, H., Zhao, X., Chen, Y., & Liu, L. (2023). Prediction of Chinese clients' satisfaction with psychotherapy by machine learning. *Frontiers in Psychiatry, 14*, 947081. https://doi.org/10.3389/fpsyt.2023.947081

Chapter 2

Scientific Philosophies and Psychodynamic Psychotherapy

Definitions

The field of psychodynamics grew up in a heady time of scientific advancement when there was the belief that everything could be understood through mechanistic explanations. Medical progress was accelerating at an astronomical rate, and psychiatric conditions were beginning to respond reliably to emerging treatments. Psychology was differentiating itself from philosophy as a science, and the topics of the mind and behavior straddled different ways that thinkers investigated the world (Gundersen, 2022, 2023): the positivistic (for our purposes, empirically based) and phenomenological (experience-based) perspectives. Psychodynamic psychotherapy (PDT) therefore has elements of both in its foundation but ultimately veered toward the unique experience between the client and therapist as its method of action. The phenomenological approach is predominant in many fields of study, like history, sociology, feminism, and gender and cultural studies. Presently, the empirical positivist perspective prevails among other areas of medicine and science, making the study of PDT an outsider compared to peers. This distinction between empirical and phenomenological paradigms is artificial and cannot capture the complexity of psychoanalytic thought but will help us enumerate the potential value of a positivist or empirical approach for the study of PDT.

Measurement

Psychoanalytic thinking in its approach is largely expectant of the truth to be *subjective* or relative to other possible explanations, despite language that is sometimes used in earlier literature about objectivity.

DOI: 10.4324/9781003323167-4

The phenomena themselves can exist *outside of observation* or sensation but can be reasoned from the experience of them or from their sequelae, like symptom behaviors. All of these products, in turn, were *determined* by psychological processes that can be uncovered with sufficient investigation, and psychoanalysis was the method with which to assess determinants. However, the processes often require a model of complexity to understand and often are overdetermined. In this way, change of an outcome is *not linear* in all instances: modifying one process, while sufficient to create change in one instance, may not show the same response in another case as other factors may support the same outcome. Shifts, additions, or deletions to one part are likely to change the whole, irreversibly and in a discontinuous fashion. Therefore, individuals must be considered from a *holistic perspective*—one in which the person is a contained system within a system of relationships and culture. The person, their experiences, and their history are inextricable from the symptom itself and must be understood in context; otherwise, the analysis potentially loses value. Even when a process is thoroughly described, it may be *specific* to which contextual variables are present and may have limited relevance to processes for other people or other times. Table 2.1 presents these concepts.

Empirical research, in its present form, accepts a view of *positivism*. This tradition suggests that an *objective truth* and natural laws exist. Only phenomena that are *observable* to all are valid—if not everyone can experience a phenomenon it is not able to be true. Observation is subjective and so contains error. We can never know the exact truth about a phenomenon because of this error, but we can learn much about the world from the patterns of error in the observation of variables. For instance, a phenomenon must exist within the margin

Table 2.1 Philosophical Differences between Psychoanalysis and Empiricism

Dimension	Psychoanalysis	Empiricism
Truth	Subjective	Objective
Observability	Not required	Required
Causality	Deterministic	Frequentist
Structure	Complexity	Reductionist
Change	Nonlinear	Linear
Context	Holistic	Contextless
Extension	Specific	Generalizable

of the error (i.e., between extreme scores, probably somewhere near the middle or central tendency), and the error of other factors can be reliably associated changes in the phenomenon (covariation or correlation). Positivism assumes a *frequentist* perspective in that value of an event is determined by its probability of occurrence (and importantly, reoccurrence), and no single experience is particularly meaningful in and of itself. Positivism is *reductionistic* in its methods for evaluation. That is, a process is isolated to its simplest relations, and then the most parsimonious conclusions are privileged over more complex explanations. Processes are assumed to be *linear* when in their simplest form. When change occurs in one phenomenon, a proportionate change in another related factor should happen as well. Associations are ideally *contextless* when truly isolated. The experimental method attempts to separate the changes in a system to only to those phenomena under investigation because if we control other sources of error through experimental manipulation, causal claims can be made about associated variables when one precedes the other in time. This contextlessness means the association is *generalizable* to other situations, and the purpose of this type of research is to predict for the "average" patient.

Significance

The power of the empirical approach is also a shortcoming. Reducing processes down to only what is observable, contextless, repeatable, and in its simplest form allows for generalization and prediction. However, it precludes a description of the full experience for any one person or persons. Psychodynamic concepts are often compressed or chopped into unintelligible or unmeaningful units. Psychotherapy occurs over a timeframe of months, inviting inputs from all sorts of factors that cannot realistically or ethically be controlled. As a result, correlations in psychotherapy process research, as in general psychology, tend to be quite small, predicting only a fraction of why a phenomenon varies. Perhaps less than 10% of why persons experience a certain outcome from therapy can be explained by factors studied in empirical research (Wampold, 2015). The rest, discarded as "residual error," is the nuance and subtlety of individual experience. Ironically, this residual variance explains the majority of the process embedded in psychotherapy and is what the psychodynamic literature expertly unpacks through clinical case study. Empirical prediction provides information about "average" patient, which is not helpful to a practicing clinician who must understand the complexity of the individual in front of them. Mathematical relations are a powerful model for understanding the world using properties everyone can derive but assumes that psychological processes follow such order, which may not be true. Many of the complex, changing, unobservable, and inferred elements commonplace in PDT may not be accurately symbolized with numbers and numerical concepts.

New Directions

What can the empirical approach add to the knowledge already known to psychoanalysis through phenomenological study? The strengths of the empirical approach lie in its iteration and systematism. A process needs to be repeated multiple times across similar conditions to be considered reportable. In this way, the relation holds up to disconfirmation and must be so robust that it will nearly always occur given the circumstances of observation. Paring down the context helps significantly with this challenge in that error is limited only to that in the variables of interest. All persons in this type of research must be treated similarly enough that they share this narrow experience of the phenomenon. Unusual observations or unique events are smoothed over by this approach so that the final relation is assumed to be a general principle applicable for every patient. In this way, the empirical approach can make predictions about a phenomenon under different circumstances, something a phenomenological approach cannot promise. Empirical research is often associated with quantitative research—investigations that rely on the enumeration of concepts and the application of mathematical principles to define relations among them. Mathematical principles then can be used as a model for understanding relations among concepts and a framework for argument that can be agreed upon by researchers with otherwise very different opinions.

So what good is empirical research for PDT? At minimum, it can provide support or disconfirmation for psychoanalytic processes but must be scrutinized closely so that operationalization and measurement match the full understanding of the ideas and concepts in psychoanalysis. It can provide order and organization to the field of PDT by emphasizing the relations that typify persons in PDT (Fonagy, 2003; Pine, 2006). It might tell us more about the typical qualities of those who will benefit or who persist in PDT (see Chapters 11 and 13). Finally, it is needed to test the efficacy and processes of PDT and provide convincing evidence of its value to those who prioritize positivist perspectives (see Chapter 3).

References

Fonagy, P. (2003). Psychoanalysis today. *World Psychiatry*, *2*(2), 73.

Gundersen, S. (2022). Mechanisms and fundamental principles in Freudian explanations. *Scandinavian Psychoanalytic Review*, *45*(2), 87–95. https://doi.org/10.1080/01062301.2023.2274145

Gundersen, S. (2023). Freud and the mind-brain problem. *The Scandinavian Psychoanalytic Review*, *46*(1–2), 4–12.

Pine, F. (2006). The psychoanalytic dictionary: A position paper on diversity and its unifiers. *Journal of the American Psychoanalytic Association*, *54*(2), 463–491.

Wampold, B. E. (2015). How important are the common factors in psychotherapy? An update. *World Psychiatry*, *14*(3), 270–277. https://doi.org/10.1002/wps.20238

Chapter 3

Outcomes in Psychodynamic Psychotherapy

Definitions

Hundreds of empirical experiments have been conducted on change in symptoms and functioning in PDT (Liliengren, 2023), and hundreds more studies of the process-outcome link. Experiments are investigations in which a group of patients receives psychodynamic psychotherapy (PDT) and another group receives a different treatment. These groups or *conditions* are measured in their outcomes and functioning pre- and posttreatment or at equivalent time intervals. Ideally from a research perspective, patients are *randomly assigned* to a condition (an algorithm or computer picks which treatment patients receive) to reduce selection bias or group differences to begin with. The amount of change or variation that occurs for patients in PDT is statistically compared to the amounts in other conditions to test whether any differences are *significant* or unlikely to be just due to chance alone (patients improving on their own). Correlational studies differ in that researchers just measure what patients and therapists normally do in their therapy. Whether variables change together (e.g., higher alliance and better outcome, and lower alliance and worse outcome) is examined statistically with a correlation coefficient, which if significant tells us there indeed is a relation and not just chance.

The results of experimental or correlational investigations can best be summarized in meta-analyses, a type of quantitative summary that can report the overall effect of a phenomenon or relation (Barber et al., 2021; Cuijpers, 2019; Norcross & Wampold, 2018). To conduct a meta-analysis, the amount of change or variation observed in each study is first standardized (an *effect-size*, in statistical language), making it comparable to the change or variation found in other studies.

DOI: 10.4324/9781003323167-5

An effect-size is an estimate of how impressive or powerful a finding is. There are many effect-size statistics based on what is being observed, but all can be judged by the arbitrary conventions of *negligible*, *small*, *medium*, and *large*, explained in Table 3.1. Effect-sizes from the different studies are then averaged to distill an overall result for the treatment or the relation under study. Meta-analysis essentially treats individual studies like a single investigation treats individual participants. In this way, we can collect the input of thousands of participants from research conducted with various populations, disorders or problems, lengths of time, assessments, and types of intervention. In this book, we will use boldface font and the conventions in Table 3.1 when we describe effect-sizes that have been established in the literature by meta-analysis.

The typical hypotheses in these meta-analyses are that PDT should show statistically significant differences in outcome that are **medium** to **large** in effect when compared to control conditions (strongly outperformed no treatment, wait-list or delay, or placebo therapy), significant **small** or **medium** differences versus standard care (indicating while we hope to improve treatment interventions, treatment-as-usual still has good efficacy), and only **negligible** to **small** differences versus other active treatments. This last prediction, that PDT will perform

Table 3.1 Effect-Size Conventions

Convention	% Better Off	% Variance Explained	Times More Likely
Negligible	.00 (50/50)	.00–.01	0.0×
Small	.08 (58/42)	.01–.09	1.4×
Medium	.19 (69/31)	.09–.25	2.2×
Large	.29 (79/21)	.25–1.00	3.8×

Note: *% Better Off* is the percentage of patients who would be more improved in the favored versus the comparison condition. The ratio beside each percent is the same expression out of 100 individuals. *% Variance Explained* is how much of patients' outcomes is attributable to being in the favored over the comparison condition. It is a theoretical value that must add up to 100% (1.00), making it useful to compare the relative contribution of multiple factors on outcome at the same time. *Times More Likely* is the number of times more likely that a patient would be improved in the favored condition for every one patient in the comparison condition (e.g., a large effect would mean that a patient in the favored group has a 4× greater chance of improvement compared to a control patient).

similarly to other therapies, may surprise some readers, especially those who have seen benefits from dynamic therapy. However, from an empirical research perspective, dynamic therapy starts from behind other evidence-based treatments. It has not had the chance to accumulate the same weight of evidence as have other treatments, nor was it developed, tested, and refined for the specific problems that outcome studies typically measure.

Measurement

Outcomes measured in empirical research of PDT have been classified by symptom reduction, patient- and therapist-defined targets, quality-of-life or well-being improvement, theoretical mechanisms change, negative outcomes and premature termination, and economic costs/benefits (Cuijpers, 2019). Symptom reduction is the most common type of outcome studied due to its measurability, distress and impairment to patients, and consistency with the medical model. Treatment-specific targets (e.g., improved relationships) and mechanisms (e.g., psychological defenses) are often more interesting to many therapists and clients. We will review studies of symptom change and economic value (treatment costs minus benefits to productivity and health service use, often over years) in this chapter and leave other chapters to examine variables of therapy process and outcome.

Symptoms may be for specific disorders or problems, diagnostic criteria met, global stress, or interpersonal or daily functioning. We cannot feature individual symptom measures here due to their enormous number but suffice it to say that researchers have expended great effort to document the reliability (the same scores for patients are achieved when measured again) and validity (scores covary with other measures of symptoms) of these instruments. Interviews with trained diagnosticians are the gold standard in empirical research because some patients might not recognize certain behaviors as symptomatic. Clients can report the presence and severity of symptoms on questionnaires, and they have often privileged knowledge of their subjective experiences. Therapist symptom descriptions are least used because clinicians may be motivated to see their clients more improved as a result of their therapy. We disagree with this last assumption because we have found therapists equally likely to be self-depreciating in their work (e.g., therapists almost always rate alliances lower than their clients; Tryon et al., 2007). Interviewer, patient, and therapist reports are only moderately correlated with one another, meaning that different perspectives largely agree on clients' problem levels but focus on different aspects of the patient.

Significance

Many meta-analyses take on different sections of the PDT outcomes literature, so much so that now meta-analyses of meta-analyses are conducted (Cuijpers, 2019; Leichsenring et al., 2022, 2023). If we had to encapsulate their conclusions, for the average patient, we can say that PDT is certainly better than doing nothing at all for the problem with **medium** to **large** effect-sizes. PDT is as good as most other accepted or evidence-supported treatments at alleviating symptoms in a timely fashion with statistically **negligible** differences. This last finding is so universal in the psychotherapy outcomes literature that researchers have named it the *dodo-bird effect* (Norcross & Wampold, 2018).

The results of meta-analyses described above included studies with short-term treatments (typically 3–4 months but less than 12; Chapter 14) with outcomes assessed at therapy termination or the study time limit. Arguably more important is how patients do in the period after they leave therapy, data which are exceptionally difficult to collect (indeed, researchers have the phrase "lost-to-follow-up" to describe this phenomenon). Patients might have real-life barriers to continuing participation like changes of address or growing families, might have sought outside treatments which blur outcomes, might be less inclined to participate if they relapse or if their treatment did not go well, and might have less of a tie to the researchers to sit through a lengthy assessment. However, we see little difference (less than a **small** effect-size) when we compare the follow-up outcomes for short-term PDT and other treatments (Barber et al., 2021; Leichsenring et al., 2022, 2023), suggesting patients retain their improvements up to 2 years following termination. In fact, some researchers believe there is evidence that patients continue to improve after completing PDT as a result of internalizing their therapist (Midgley et al., 2021), something called the *sleeper effect*.

There is similar evidence for the effectiveness of long-term PDT, defined here as psychodynamic or psychoanalytic therapy (once or twice weekly) lasting longer than one year. The way we research long-term treatments differs in study design and diminishes the effect-size estimates we can see for long-term PDT. Given the extended study duration, a no-treatment control would be unethical. Long-term PDT is almost always compared to an effective therapy (treatment-as-usual, another longer-term treatment, or short-term treatments) so no one is left without at least some therapy. Differences in outcome at the end of the study period shrink because long-term PDT is up against an active treatment (as opposed to no treatment). Additionally, patients in longer-term PDT may have difficulty experiencing change, as longer-term treatments in empirical research are generally for persons with more intractable or pervasive difficulties, like chronic depression or personality disorder. In everyday practice, long-term PDT is more likely to include persons with all sorts of reasons for seeking treatment. Nevertheless, several meta-analyses have showed **small** to **medium** effect-sizes for longer-term treatments up to several years out (Barber et al., 2021; Leichsenring et al., 2022, 2023). One meta-analysis reviewed investigations of outcomes in psychoanalysis specifically (de Maat et al., 2013). Fourteen studies were found with 605 patients undergoing three or more sessions per week and a median duration of 4 years. Good efficacy was seen for a mixed set of disorders, but only one of the trials compared patients in psychoanalysis to patients in another group so we cannot tell how patients would have fared over that same time period without psychoanalysis.

Other meta-analyses have reviewed evidence for PDT with specific disorders or populations. We can say PDT is a viable option for depressive disorders, anxiety disorders (including panic, social, or generalized anxiety), psychosomatic conditions, substance use disorders, and mixed personality disorders (Barber et al., 2021; Leichsenring et al., 2023). Preliminary but insufficient evidence exists to draw conclusions about the efficacy of PDT for schizophrenia, bipolar, obsessive-compulsive, and posttraumatic stress disorders. For posttraumatic stress disorder, several groups have developed new PDT treatments and have begun testing them (Brand et al., 2022; Busch et al., 2021; Leichsenring et al., 2021). Recently, studies accumulated to test the efficacy of dynamic therapy in children and adolescents (Midgley et al., 2021). PDT has a **medium**-sized effect for internalizing disorders and early experiences of adversity or trauma and a significant but **small**-sized effect for externalizing disorders (see Chapter 21).

Like all methods of inquiry, meta-analysis is susceptible to shortcomings that contextualize what we can conclude. The number of studies ultimately included in meta-analyses is almost always tiny relative to the literature that the researchers review (e.g., 6% for Leichsenring et al., 2023). Literature search strategy (e.g., search terms and dates reviewed) and inclusion/exclusion criteria for individual studies are now preregistered with an international research body and included in the publication of the review. Second, the quality of research studies going into a meta-analysis determines the trustworthiness of the result ("garbage in, garbage out," researchers say). Many researchers offer quality checks as part of their meta-analyses, ranking the individual studies by their methods and stating the risk of bias. Thoma and colleagues (2012) directly put the quality of outcome research on PDT and other treatments to the test on 22 different standards and found four decades of research produced similar quality work regardless of orientation. Third, some types of meta-analyses ("network meta-analyses") mathematically "fill-in" studies that never were conducted (for our purposes, head-to-head trials of PDT vs. other active treatments). Thoma and coworkers (2012) found only 7 out of 207 trials (3%) actually compared PDT and CBT in the same study. Network meta-analyses are used to make conclusions about how the treatments "would" perform. These results skirt the observational method, are weighted toward treatments with a larger existing evidence base, and reduce the likelihood that researchers are to carry out the needed studies in reality (Keefe, 2015).

New Directions

Dissemination or *implementation* are initiatives to transport treatments validated by research into practice settings (Chambers et al., 2013). Empirically supported therapies almost never appear to perform as well in the community as compared to the university, a finding so routine that it is called the *voltage drop*. Additionally, *program drift* is when practitioners' adherence to a specific therapy protocol invariably diminishes over time in naturalistic settings, especially when patients have pressing needs or funding for the research collaboration leaves. To avoid these potential pitfalls, Gibbons and colleagues (2016) attempted a community-focused approach to implementing PDT in a practice setting. They first spent time developing relationships with program directors, therapists, and community clients. They asked these stakeholders what they would want from research, identifying priorities such as continuing education, relationship training, cultural competence, and helping practitioners support communities. They adapted

PDT by increasing the alliance focus and giving therapists specific training in alliance development, incorporating cultural sensitivity, and focusing on socialization as a way to engage patients in treatment. Their research program, published with community coauthors, showed therapists were able to learn PDT, execute it well, and had greater outcomes in treating depression than treatment-as-usual and equivalent outcomes to CBT taught to the same therapists (Gibbons et al., 2016).

References

Barber, J. P., Muran, J. C., McCarthy, K. S., Keefe, J. R., & Zilcha-Mano, S. (2021). Research on dynamic therapies. In M. Barkham, W. Lutz, & L. G. Castonguay (Eds.), *Handbook of psychotherapy and behavior change* (6th ed., pp. 443–494). Wiley.

Brand, B. L., Schielke, H., Schiavone, F., & Lanius, R. A. (2022). *Finding solid ground: Overcoming obstacles in trauma treatment*. Oxford University Press.

Busch, F., Milrod, B., Chen, C., & Singer, M. (2021). *Trauma focused psychodynamic psychotherapy: A step-by-step treatment manual*. Oxford University Press.

Chambers, D. A., Glasgow, R. E., & Stange, K. C. (2013). The dynamic sustainability framework: Addressing the paradox of sustainment amid ongoing change. *Implementation Science*, *8*(117). https://doi.org/10.1186/1748-5908-8-117

Cuijpers, P. (2019). Targets and outcomes of psychotherapies for mental disorders: An overview. *World Psychiatry*, *18*(3), 276–285. https://doi.org/10.1002/wps.20682

de Maat, S., de Jonghe, F., de Kraker, R., Leichsenring, F., Abbass, A., Luyten, P., Barber, J. P., Van, R., & Dekker, J. (2013). The current state of the empirical evidence for psychoanalysis: A meta-analytic approach. *Harvard Review of Psychiatry*, *21*(3), 107–137. https://doi.org/10.1097/HRP.0b013e318294f5fd

Gibbons, M. B. C., Gallop, R., Thompson, D., Luther, D., Crits-Christoph, K., Jacobs, J., & Crits-Christoph, P. (2016). Comparative effectiveness of cognitive therapy and dynamic psychotherapy for major depressive disorder in a community mental health setting: A randomized clinical noninferiority trial. *JAMA Psychiatry*, *73*(9), 904–912. https://doi.org/10.1001/jamapsychiatry.2016.1720

Keefe, J. R. (2015). Heightened risk of false positives in a network meta-analysis of social anxiety. *Lancet Psychiatry*, *2*(4), 292–293. https://doi.org/10.1016/S2215-0366(15)00043-7

Leichsenring, F., Abbass, A., Heim, N., Keefe, J. R., Kisely, S., Luyten, P., & Steinert, C. (2023). The status of psychodynamic psychotherapy as an empirically supported treatment for common mental disorders–An umbrella review based on updated criteria. *World Psychiatry*, *22*(2), 286–304. https://doi.org/10.1002/wps.21041

Leichsenring, F., Steinert, C., Beutel, M. E., Feix, L., Gündel, H., Hermann, A., Karabatsiakis, A., Knaevelsrud, C., König, H.-H., Kolassa, I. T., Kruse, J., Niemeyer, H., Nöske, F., Palmer, S., Peters, E., Reese, J.-P., Reuss, A., Salzer, S., Schade-Brittinger, C., Schuster, P., Stark, R., Weidner, K., von Wietersheim, J., Witthöft, M., Wöller, W., & Hoyer, J. (2020). Trauma-focused psychodynamic therapy and STAIR Narrative Therapy of post-traumatic stress disorder related to childhood maltreatment: Trial protocol of a multicentre randomised controlled trial assessing psychological, neuro-biological and health economic outcomes (ENHANCE). *BMJ Open*, 10(12), e040123. https://doi.org/10.1136/bmjopen-2020-040123

Leichsenring, F., Steinert, C., Rabung, S., & Ioannidis, J. P. (2022). The efficacy of psychotherapies and pharmacotherapies for mental disorders in adults: An umbrella review and meta-analytic evaluation of recent meta-analyses. *World Psychiatry*, 21(1), 133–145. https://doi.org/10.1002/wps.20933

Lilliengren, P. (2023). A comprehensive overview of randomized controlled trials of psychodynamic psychotherapies. *Psychoanalytic Psychotherapy*, 37(2), 117–140. https://doi.org/10.1080/02668734.2023.2197617

Midgley, N., Mortimer, R., Cirasola, A., Batra, P., & Kennedy, E. (2021). The evidence-base for psychodynamic psychotherapy with children and adolescents: A narrative synthesis. *Frontiers in Psychology*, 12, 662671. https://doi.org/10.3389/fpsyg.2021.662671

Norcross, J. C., & Wampold, B. E. (2018). A new therapy for each patient: Evidence-based relationships and responsiveness. *Journal of Clinical Psychology*, 74(11), 1889–1906. https://doi.org/10.1002/jclp.22678

Thoma, N. C., McKay, D., Gerber, A. J., Milrod, B. L., Edwards, A. R., & Kocsis, J. H. (2012). A quality-based review of randomized controlled trials of cognitive-behavioral therapy for depression: An assessment and metar-egression. *American Journal of Psychiatry*, 169(1), 22–30.

Tryon, G. S., Blackwell, S. C., & Hammel, E. F. (2007). A meta-analytic exami-nation of client-therapist perspectives of the working alliance. *Psychotherapy Research*, 17(6), 629–642. https://doi.org/10.1080/10503300701320611

Part II

Therapeutic Relationship

Evidence in Psychodynamic Psychotherapy: A Contemporary Introduction

Chapter 4

Transference in Psychodynamic Psychotherapy

Definitions

The concept of transference is perhaps the most central principle and tool of psychodynamic psychotherapy (PDT) and theory. It is patients' unconscious projection of past feelings and perceptions onto their present-day therapist, affording a window into their experience and into how they may come across to others in their everyday life and relationships (Levy & Scala, 2012; Zepf, 2010). These repeated patterns come about early in patients' lives to handle conflict and anxiety and later become habitual to the patient, even when painful or no longer effective. Therapists comment on their observation of transference as a way for patients to gain insight about their interactional patterns and to become more comfortable with authentic expression and behavior (see Chapter 10). Transference specifically refers to replay of these patterns with the therapist *as if* they were an ordinary person in the patient's life. *Extratransference* is the repetition of relationships outside of the therapy (e.g., with romantic partners, family, and friends) (Levy & Scala, 2012; Zepf, 2010).

Transference is the precursor to the development of what is analyzed in psychoanalysis, the *transference neurosis.* A subtle but impactful distinction, it is when past conflicts are replaced with a new, current conflict that is acted out with the therapist *as* an important person in the patient's life (Levy & Scala, 2012; Zepf, 2010). Themes in the transference neurosis can be the same as in the transference, but the intensity and object are different. In its most powerful manifestation, the treatment becomes everything for the patient—all thoughts, feelings, and behaviors now include the therapist. An example might be an avoidant patient and their therapist contemplating increasing the

DOI: 10.4324/9781003323167-7

frequency of therapy. The patient might experience inexplicable anger toward the therapist for "making" them want more sessions. Here, the patient's frustration over becoming dependent in relationships now is with the therapist. The patient may recognize the feeling and know the therapist's intent but cannot help engaging in the repeated cycle. A transference neurosis shows that the treatment has had an effect on the patient as the therapist is now a participant in the patient's typical style of relating. Transference neurosis is brought about by therapeutic interventions (e.g., free association, focusing inward, therapeutic abstinence and neutrality, and interpretation; Chapter 10), enabling such to be treated in the space (Levy & Scala, 2012; Zepf, 2010). For a patient's real-world behaviors (their extratransference) to change, those same patterns must enter into the therapy room. When the symptom is worked through within the therapeutic relationship, it will subsequently also change within the patient's external relationships. The provision of supportive interventions (e.g., gratification, containment, and active problem-solving; Chapter 9) reduces the likelihood of a full transference neurosis. PDT, which makes more use of supportive techniques than psychoanalysis, works with the transference and extratransference. Psychotherapy research, and also then this text, is less able to speak to the development and analysis of the transference neurosis but certainly can add to an understanding of transference and extratransference.

Three research traditions have emerged in defining the construct of transference: ego psychology, interpersonal, and social-cognitive theories. Ego psychology proposes conflict between internal motivation versus what is actual, possible, or proper in the real world. The ego or self defends against conflict unconsciously by turning unacceptable wishes into more socially palatable behaviors but registers the presence of conflict with *signal anxiety*. Studies show that the brain and body learn to respond to threat events (e.g., pairing of familiar facial images and electric shock) even when participants are not aware they are being triggered (Wong, 1999). Patients frequently come to therapy with the conscious sense something is wrong but uncertainty of what that might be. Repeated patterns or symptom behaviors in response to signal anxiety are forms of transference.

Interpersonal theory conceptualizes personality as the reoccurring situations in which individuals find themselves. Transference is when individuals engage in repeated patterns of integrating (prosocial) or disintegrating (antisocial) behaviors in an attempt to satisfy various biological and psychological tensions or needs (e.g., thirst, tenderness, or anxiety) with others, called *dynamisms.* Empirical researchers proposed the *interpersonal circumplex* model (Horowitz et al., 1993) mapping relational experiences on two perpendicular dimensions: affiliation–hostility and dominance–submission. All interpersonal behaviors encompass some combination of the two dimensions (e.g., a person showing respect to a parent evinces submissive caring, wanting both to defer and be close to the other). The characteristic way that individuals interact with others on these two dimensions represents transference in this model.

The social-cognitive model of transference comes out of an information-processing perspective (Andersen & Przybylinski, 2012). Using a computer metaphor, the human brain accepts sensory input about relationships, encodes experiences, and stores information for later retrieval. In meeting a new individual, information is interpreted through previously internalized constructs of past relationships. *Representation-derived inferences* to this new individual are an amalgamation of both new and old information, with past experiences of others being used to fill in or explain behavior. Transference is a cognitive shortcut that allows more efficient, but biased, information processing of social relationships. Unlike other perspectives of transference, the social-cognitive model does not rely on motives or drives and is more concerned with cognitive structure and function (reducing complexity and effortful processing) than with meaning and experience. Tested in mostly undergraduate samples, the implication of a social-cognitive model of transference is that the way clients interact with clinicians is influenced by already-existent mental representations of others.

Measurement

Therapists often recognize the transference in therapy when patients respond to them in an unexpected or seemingly extreme way for the situation, reflecting past experiences for which that behavior was a solution to unconscious conflict. Taking advantage of therapists' proficiency in identifying transference, some measurement tools simply ask the therapist to rate the transference in a session. Therapists can complete a common three-item questionnaire that asks the amount of negative, positive, and overall transference that occurred in a session (Graff & Luborsky, 1977). The *Missouri Identifying Transference Scale* (Multon et al., 1996) is a more comprehensive therapist-rated instrument assessing patient reactions (e.g., admiration, clinging, anger, and mistrust) experienced in the therapy. Two subscales provide levels of negative and positive transference.

Similarly, clients can rate transference when asked about the repeated problems and experiences in their relationships. The *Inventory of Interpersonal Problems* (IIP; Horowitz et al., 1993) uses the interpersonal circumplex model to typify eight types of conflicts that patients characteristically have trouble doing in relationships or do too much of with others (domineering, intrusive, overagreeing, exploitable, submissive, avoidant, cold, and vindictive). Clients rate the IIP for their relationships in general. Unless the client thinks to include the therapist as part of their ratings, the IIP is largely a measure of extratransference.

Other ways of measuring transference require repeated observations of the patient's relationships, many times through client interviews or therapy session recordings. In the Core Conflictual Relationship Theme (CCRT, Luborsky & Crits-Christoph, 1998) method, narratives about interpersonal interactions are qualitatively coded for the presence of (a) wishes or needs the patient has, (b) what others do in response to these wishes, and (c) the patient's resulting affect and behavior. The most frequent of these wishes and responses make up the CCRT formulation (e.g., to be perfect, feeling criticized, being angry and overcontrolling as a result) by the premise that the transferential pattern should be the most repeated in the patient's relationships. The Structural Analysis of Social Behavior (SASB; Critchfield & Benjamin, 2024) method assesses specific utterances or behaviors in client interactions for their degree of affiliation–hostility (love–hate) and interdependence–independence (enmeshment–differentiation) on each of three surfaces (focus: self, other, or introject). The combination of these dimensions and focuses portrays the internal representation or *copy process* the client is using in the interaction (e.g., the person ignores, the other walls-off, and the person learns self-neglect). Both methods have self-report questionnaires that clients can complete to provide the data without the need for observational coding. These methods will assess only extratransference unless the patient includes interactions with the therapist specifically.

Significance

The adult and child psychotherapy case literature situates the origin of transference in early interactions with significant others. Surprisingly, no empirical research has been published that directly examines the link from identifiable developmental experiences to transference later in the therapy setting (but see Chapter 17 on attachment). An exception is Luborsky and colleagues (1998) who demonstrated transference could be assessed from children's narratives ages 3 to 5 years. Interpersonal patterns were observable across this period but were more positive and less stable than in adults and restricted to a smaller set of interpersonal themes.

Empirical research has demonstrated that transference occurs automatically in everyday life (Andersen & Przybylinski, 2012). In experiments typical to the social-cognitive model, participants come into the laboratory and write sentences about qualities of a significant other. Researchers create composites of potential persons with information from participants' own or others' narratives. The same participants return two weeks later and are given descriptions of potential partners for what they believe is a separate experiment. Participants' reactions to these stories suggest the operation of transference. Participants express more positive and negative emotions to depictions of others who are more similar in ways to important people in their lives. They show stronger preferences to meet and work with familiar persons and predict that their relationships would last longer. Importantly, when asked to recall the descriptions of or interact with someone assumed to be the person described, they remember or fill in erroneous details relevant to their significant others (Andersen & Przybylinski, 2012).

Transference toward the therapist is active even prior to treatment. Clients' representations of others (e.g., expected hostility, independence, or love from others) measured before they meet their therapists predicted the strength of their relationship with their therapists two months into treatment with **large** effect-sizes (Zilcha-Mano et al., 2014). Transference has been measured during treatment to show development over therapy. Transference reactions, defined as similarity of interaction themes with the therapist in the session to themes reported for outside relationships, occurred for three-quarters of patients as early as Session 3 and comprised 16% of content in the beginning of therapy and 22% near the end of treatment (Luborsky & Crits-Christoph, 1998). The few studies examining transference over short- and longer-term therapy report positive transference toward the therapist and others remains stable or increases over the therapy, whereas negative transference increases, peaks, and declines by the end of more successful treatments (Blatt et al., 1996). The ratio of positive and negative transference themes increases over treatment, such that most patients have relatively more positive content in their relationship representations.

Finally, research has produced pictures of how transference functions in the brain. Healthy controls gave narratives that were then coded their CCRT (Loughhead et al., 2010). The same persons participated in brain scans and showed greater activation in areas processing autobiographical memory, sense of self, and emotion when presented with narratives from their own CCRT than others'. In another study, healthy controls identified a personal characteristic, related a formative memory connected with it, and picked an image associated with their story (Wade-Bohleber et al., 2019). Later they were exposed to those meaningful pictures and other images while undergoing brain scans. Again, there was greater activation in areas implicated in autobiographical memory, consciousness and self, and emotion. The same methodology was used in healthy and depressed persons with or without a history of trauma (Wade-Bohleber et al., 2020). All participants exhibited greater brain activation in areas for autobiographical memory, sense of self, and emotion. Areas controlling emotion inhibition showed *reduced* activity in persons with depression and *increased* activation in individuals with early adversity, suggesting depressed persons have trouble regulating emotion and rumination in response to transference cues and persons with trauma have numbing or self-distancing reactions.

New Directions

While most of the manualized, evidenced-based PDTs show a light touch on transference, transference-focused psychotherapy (TFP) showcases the impact that transference holds in the space of PDT (Kernberg et al., 2008). To promote transference to its deepest potential, TFP is less focused on providing supportive interventions and instead concentrates on delivering transference interpretations from the initiation of therapy. This creates a unique and specific avenue for engaging with transference compared to other PDTs. The therapist uses the alliance to exemplify how relational dynamics may be unfolding for the patient, creating insight that aims to facilitate stronger, more stable relationships in the patient's real life. Outcomes showed that TFP was effective for difficult-to-treat conditions like borderline and narcissistic personality (Kernberg et al., 2008) and worked by improving attachment security (Chapter 17) and ability to think about self and others (Chapter 19).

References

Andersen, S. M., & Przybylinski, E. (2012). Experiments on transference in interpersonal relations: Implications for treatment. *Psychotherapy, 49*(3), 370.

Blatt, S. J., Stayner, D. A., Auerbach, J. S., & Behrends, R. S. (1996). Change in object and self-representations in long-term, intensive, inpatient treatment of seriously disturbed adolescents and young adults. *Psychiatry, 59*(1), 82–107.

Critchfield, K. L., & Benjamin, L. S. (2024). *Structural Analysis of Social Behavior (SASB): A primer for clinical use.* American Psychological Association.

Graff, H., & Luborsky, L. (1977). Long-term trends in transference and resistance: A report on a quantitative-analytic method applied to four psychoanalyses. *Journal of the American Psychoanalytic Association, 25*(2), 471–490.

Horowitz, L. M., Rosenberg, S. E., & Bartholomew, K. (1993). Interpersonal problems, attachment styles, and outcome in brief dynamic psychotherapy. *Journal of Consulting and Clinical Psychology, 61*(4), 549–560. https://doi.org/10.1037/0022-006X.61.4.549

Kernberg, O. F., Yeomans, F. E., Clarkin, J. F., & Levy, K. N. (2008). Transference focused psychotherapy: Overview and update. *The International Journal of Psychoanalysis, 89*(3), 601–620.

Levy, K. N., & Scala, J. W. (2012). Transference, transference interpretations, and transference-focused psychotherapies. *Psychotherapy, 49*(3), 391–403. https://doi.org/10.1037/a0029371

Loughhead, J. W., Luborsky, L., Weingarten, C. P., Krause, E. D., German, R. E., Kirk, D., & Gur, R. C. (2010). Brain activation during autobiographical relationship episode narratives: A core conflictual relationship theme approach. *Psychotherapy Research, 20*(5), 607–617. https://doi.org/10.1080/10503300903470735

Luborsky, L., & Crits-Christoph, P. (1998). *Understanding transference: The core conflictual relationship theme method.* Basic Books.

Multon, K. D., Patton, M. J., & Kivlighan, D. M., Jr. (1996). Development of the Missouri Identifying Transference Scale. *Journal of Counseling Psychology, 43*(3), 243–252. https://doi.org/10.1037/0022-0167.43.3.243

Wade-Bohleber, L. M., Boeker, H., Ernst, J., Grimm, S., Brügger, N., Berwian, I. M., Vetter, J., Preller, K. H., Himmighoffen, H., Kleim, B., Seifritz, E., & Richter, A. (2019). Thinking about the past to shape the present: Neural activation during the recall of relationship episodes. *Behavioural Brain Research, 359*, 783–791. https://doi.org/10.1016/j.bbr.2018.11.018

Wade-Bohleber, L. M., Boeker, H., Grimm, S., Gärtner, M., Ernst, J., Recher, D. A., Buergi, N., Seifritz, E., & Richter, A. (2020). Depression is associated with hyperconnectivity of an introspective socio-affective network during the recall of formative relationship episodes. *Journal of Affective Disorders*, *274*, 522–534. https://doi.org/10.1016/j.jad.2020.05.010

Wong, P. S. (1999). Anxiety, signal anxiety, and unconscious anticipation: Neuroscientific evidence for an unconscious signal function in humans. *Journal of the American Psychoanalytic Association*, *47*(3), 817–841. https://doi.org/10.1177/00030651990470031901

Zepf, S. (2010). The psychoanalytic process and Freud's concepts of transference and transference neurosis. *Psychoanalytic Psychology*, *27*(1), 55.

Zilcha-Mano, S., McCarthy, K. S., Dinger, U., & Barber, J. P. (2014). To what extent is alliance affected by transference? An empirical exploration. *Psychotherapy*, *51*(3), 424.

Chapter 5

Countertransference in Psychodynamic Psychotherapy

Definitions

Countertransference is the therapist's own feelings and behaviors toward a patient, often unconsciously evoked by interactions between the two in the therapeutic space. The classical conceptualization (the *narrow* perspective, Gabbard, 2020; Hayes et al., 2018) posited these feelings were born out of the analyst's own childhood conflicts, interfered with objective perception of the patient, and needed to be worked through in supervision, setting the stage for the tripartite model of psychoanalytic training (academics, supervision, and personal therapy). Cultural countertransference, or therapists' reactions to clients due to formative social messaging in their background about race, gender, or other identity factors, can be included as an example of this viewpoint (see Chapter 22).

Later psychodynamic thinking broadened countertransference to be any reaction of the therapist to the patient. Countertransference in this *totalistic* perspective (Gabbard, 2020; Hayes et al., 2018) could be a useful clinical avenue when managed. Winnicott (1947) normalized negative countertransference feelings (as opposed to prioritizing the therapist's comfort in the treatment) and described how acceptance of negative emotions honors a patient's needs, despite being unreasonable at times. Later in the therapy, the therapist's feelings need to be revealed for analysis to be complete so that the patient can understand how they have influenced others negatively in development without awareness and process the experience of being supported through this.

The *complementary* perspective is that the patient's dynamics pull the therapist to react as a counterpart to the patient in a characteristic way (Hayes et al., 2018). Enactment is inevitable, and the therapist helps the patient work through this transference–countertransference

DOI: 10.4324/9781003323167-8

expression together. Certain personality styles in a patient will engender the same types of feelings and reactions in all clinicians (Winnicott's [1947] "objective countertransference") and will not be idiosyncratic to the therapist's own conflicts. For example, patients with depressive personality styles (often self-punitive, holding unrealistically high standards) frequently elicit more positive countertransference among therapists (feelings of collaboration and a desire to help), whereas those with borderline personality styles (often unpredictable, vacillating between intense mood states, and expecting abandonment) commonly bring about feelings of frustration and helplessness within a therapist (Betan et al., 2005; Rossberg et al., 2007; Øvstebø et al., 2023). Similar feelings and responses are likely experienced by others in those patients' lives, reinforcing that countertransference feelings can be an expectable reaction to a patient's transference behaviors and an informative indicator in the therapy (Colli et al., 2014).

A common criticism of many CT perspectives is they neglect the therapist's contribution to the way the patient behaves in treatment (Hayes et al., 2018). Recent thinking suggests countertransference is jointly created by both patient and therapist and involves the therapist's reactions to the patient, informed by their own internal workings. For example, higher client attachment anxiety levels have been associated with decreases in therapist parental countertransference over therapy, perhaps feeling less needed (Westerling et al., 2019). Therapists, however, reported more overwhelmed feelings across time as client attachment anxiety decreased. This *integrative* perspective emphasizes the therapist's role and responsibility in such reactions (Hayes et al., 2018), challenges the notion of therapist abstinence and objectivity, and presages the ascendance of the real relationship as an important component of therapy (see Chapter 8).

Measurement

Like transference, countertransference may take any form and so is frequently discussed in the abstract. Self-report questionnaires like the *Therapist Response Questionnaire* (Betan et al., 2005) or *Feeling Checklist* (Falkenström et al., 2024) collect therapists' attitudes toward their clients in general, which then can be compared to those therapists' responses to specific patients to see if the therapist departs from their normal reactions to clients. Other measures look for the cooccurrence of conflict-laden adjectives in therapist's descriptions of themselves and their ratings of several of their clients (McClure & Hodge, 1987). In still other measures, supervisors or observers have been asked to rate the therapist's countertransference style based on in-session behaviors, like the *Inventory of Countertransference Behaviors* (Friedman & Gelso, 2000).

Another route that has been suggested is to borrow from measures of transference to formulate the therapists' own characteristic interpersonal style. The Core Conflictual Relationship Theme method (CCRT; see Chapter 4) captures interpersonal patterns repeated across relationships in patients' narratives and can be applied to therapists as well. Tishby and Wiseman (2022) asked therapists to compose narratives describing interactions with their parents as well as their clients and coded these stories with the CCRT method. Table 5.1 displays six types of countertransference toward clients in reference to their parents' responses. Similarly, the Social Analysis of Social Behavior (SASB; see Chapter 5) method has been used to measure how therapists relate to themselves and their own expectations of others as a function of therapy (Nissen-Lie et al., 2015). Finally, therapists' attachment styles

Table 5.1 Countertransference Themes and Management Techniques

Countertransference Themes		Countertransference Management Techniques (Hayes et al., 2018)
Self-Report (Nissen-Lie et al., 2015)	Narratives (Tishby & Wiseman, 2022)	
Overwhelmed/ disorganized	Same wishes toward parents and client	Understanding self and own reactions
Helpless/inadequate	Perceive client response like parents'	Understanding clients and conceptualizing behaviors
Positive		
Special/overinvolved		
Sexualized	React to clients like how responded to parents	Empathy toward clients' suffering
Disengaged		
Parental/protective	React to clients like how own parents responded	Self-integration, genuineness, and wholeness
Criticized/mistreated		
	Attempted to repair ruptures with clients opposite to parents' responses	Anxiety management strategies for therapist

have been used to approximate countertransference. Their impact on therapy will be covered in Chapter 17.

In-session behaviors that therapists utilize to become aware of, mitigate, or harness their feelings productively can be measured with the *Countertransference Management Scale* (Pérez-Rojas et al., 2017). Actions like having empathy for patients evoking strong countertransference or being able to view negative behavior as a symptom that has yet to be successfully treated, and not a personal attack on the therapist, can greatly assist in maintenance of the therapeutic alliance and quality of treatment. This instrument captures therapist behaviors and process events based on five theoretical mechanisms given in Table 5.1.

Significance

Countertransference is often an unconscious process, and recognition requires continual self-reflection by the clinician and awareness of one's own internal conflicts. There have been positive correlations between levels of countertransference awareness and hours spent in psychotherapy or supervision, mindful practices, and positive self-attitude (Hayes et al., 2018). Interestingly, trainees showed more countertransference awareness and less impulsivity in response to clinical vignettes than very experienced therapists (Normandin & Bouchard, 1993), perhaps due to more recent supervision experiences. However, trainees still are likely to underreport negative feelings of countertransference (Mohr et al., 2005). Honesty and willingness to disclose countertransference reactions is dependent on trainees' perception of how open their supervisors seem to be to the topic (Ponton & Sauerheber, 2014). This finding was particularly heightened in supervisees' interactions with their supervisors when controversial political material entered the therapy (McCarthy et al., 2022).

Countertransference, when recognized, can be used in conceptualization and treatment planning. Being able to attribute certain countertransference feelings to distinct personality presentations can be a helpful diagnostic indicator and evidence in support of a formulation (Betan et al., 2005; Colli et al., 2014; Rossberg et al., 2007). For example, those with an obsessional personality style wish for perfection, blame others for obstruction, and are left feeling angry and shameful as a result. Clinicians often experience a power struggle and disengagement in the room due to tedious discussions of intellectual material (Colli et al., 2014) as opposed to genuine exploration and toleration of affect.

Countertransference influences process and outcome throughout the therapy. Negative therapist reactions (e.g., frustration, withdrawal, and helplessness) relate to lower alliances, more ruptures without resolution, early dropout, and less successful treatment (Hayes et al., 2018; Ovstebo et al., 2023; Rocco et al., 2021; Rossberg et al., 2007; Tishby & Wiseman, 2022). Positive countertransference (e.g., pride, liking, and helpfulness) showed several complex relations with these processes. Positive countertransference led to smoother but more superficial sessions (Markin et al., 2013). Professional self-doubt predicted outcome when therapists also experienced a positive orientation toward themselves on the SASB (Nissen-Lie et al., 2015). When therapists used positive behaviors to repair negative patterns similar to their own history (i.e., provided an opposite response to what they themselves experienced in the past), they in fact saw more ruptures (Tishby & Wiseman, 2022).

The existence of countertransference does not mean the therapy is less likely to be successful. Being able to work through these feelings, particularly activating or difficult ones, may be a key piece to competent practice and favorable treatment outcomes. Countertransference management has shown to have a **large** effect on positive treatment outcome, and greater use of these skills related to fewer undesired expressions of countertransference experienced by therapists (Friedman & Gelso, 2000; Hayes et al., 2018), which may slow down the process and make use of countertransference more purposive. Change over treatment in one type of countertransference, decreasing therapist's sense of helplessness, was related to improvement in personality symptoms in a long-term treatment, perhaps as the therapist felt more in control or familiar with their countertransference (Øvstebø et al., 2023).

New Directions

Countertransference is probably an interaction between therapist and client characteristics, real and in the past. At the same time, personality styles and attachment bring out predictable countertransferences that when aware can aid in formulation and treatment planning. Negative countertransference (hostility and disengagement) rarely relates to good therapy, and positive countertransference, while weakly related to changes in the therapy, can be misleading or exist in complex relation to other process factors. Management of countertransference seems to be the way to handle this inevitable experience in the therapy for successful outcome. Supervision is obviously helpful, and new research-based training like Facilitative Interaction Skills (Anderson et al., 2016) or Deliberate Practice (Rousmaniere, 2016) could prove instructive. Interestingly, countertransference has entered into the therapeutic lexicon and is commonly discussed in cognitive-behavioral therapy circles (Prasko et al., 2010).

References

Anderson, T., Crowley, M. E. J., Himawan, L., Holmberg, J. K., & Uhlin, B. D. (2016). Therapist facilitative interpersonal skills and training status: A randomized clinical trial on alliance and outcome. *Psychotherapy Research*, *26*(5), 511–529.

Betan, E., Heim, A. K., Zittel-Conklin, C., & Westen, D. (2005). Countertransference phenomena and personality pathology in clinical practice: An empirical investigation. *American Journal of Psychiatry*, *162*(5), 890–898.

Colli, A., Tanzilli, A., Dimaggio, G., & Lingiardi, V. (2014). Patient personality and therapist response: An empirical investigation. *American Journal of Psychiatry*, *171*(1), 102–108.

Falkenström, F., Bjerén, J., Björklund, F., Holmqvist, R., & Ekeblad, A. (2024). Patient attachment and reflective functioning as predictors for therapist in-session feelings. *Journal of Counseling Psychology*, 71(3), 190–201. https://doi.org/10.1037/cou0000726

Friedman, S. M., & Gelso, C. J. (2000). The development of the inventory of countertransference behavior. *Journal of Clinical Psychology*, *56*(9), 1221–1235.

Gabbard, G. O. (2020). The role of countertransference in contemporary psychiatric treatment. *World Psychiatry*, *19*(2), 243–244. https://doi.org/10.1002/wps.20746

Hayes, J. A., Gelso, C. J., Goldberg, S., & Kivlighan, D. M. (2018). Countertransference management and effective psychotherapy: Meta-analytic findings. *Psychotherapy*, *55*(4), 496–507. https://doi.org/10.1037/pst0000189

Markin, R. D., McCarthy, K., & Barber, J. P. (2013). Transference, countertransference, emotional expression, and session quality over the course of supportive expressive therapy: The raters' perspective. *Psychotherapy Research*, *23*(2), 213–228. https://doi.org/10.1080/10503307.2012.747013

McCarthy, K. S., Capone, C., Davidtz, J., & Solomonov, N. (2022). The association between political climate and trainees' supervision experiences and needs. *The Clinical Supervisor*, *41*(2), 107–126.

McClure, B. A., & Hodge, R. W. (1987). Measuring countertransference and attitude in therapeutic relationships. *Psychotherapy: Theory, Research, Practice, Training*, *24*(3), 325–335.

Mohr, J. J., Gelso, C. J., & Hill, C. E. (2005). Client and counselor trainee attachment as predictors of session evaluation and countertransference behavior in first counseling sessions. *Journal of Counseling Psychology*, *52*(3), 298.

Nissen-Lie, H. A., Rønnestad, M. H., Høglend, P. A., Havik, O. E., Solbakken, O. A., Stiles, T. C., & Monsen, J. T. (2015). Love yourself as a person, doubt yourself as a therapist? *Clinical Psychology & Psychotherapy.* https://doi.org/10.1002/cpp.1977

Normandin, L., & Bouchard, M.-A. (1993). The effects of theoretical orientation and experience on rational, reactive and reflective countertransference. *Psychotherapy Research, 3,* 77–94. https://doi.org/10.1080/1050330931233 1333689.

Øvstebø, R. B., Pedersen, G., Wilberg, T., Røssberg, J. I., Dahl, H. S. J., & Kvarstein, E. H. (2023). Countertransference in the treatment of patients with personality disorders: A longitudinal study. *Psychotherapy Research, 34*(8), 1051–1065. https://doi.org/10.1080/10503307.2023.2279645.

Pérez-Rojas, A. E., Palma, B., Bhatia, A., Jackson, J., Norwood, E., Hayes, J. A., & Gelso, C. J. (2017). The development and initial validation of the countertransference management scale. *Psychotherapy, 54*(3), 307–319. https://doi.org/10.1037/pst0000126

Ponton, R. F., & Sauerheber, J. D. (2014). Supervisee countertransference: A holistic supervision approach. *Counselor Education and Supervision, 53*(4), 254–266.

Prasko, J., Diveky, T., Grambal, A., Kamaradova, D., Mozny, P., Sigmundova, Z., & Vyskocilova, J. (2010). Transference and countertransference in cognitive behavioral therapy. *Biomedical Papers, 154*(3), 189–197.

Rocco, D., De Bei, F., Negri, A., & Filipponi, L. (2021). The relationship between self-observed and other-observed countertransference and session outcome. *Psychotherapy, 58*(2), 301–309. https://doi.org/10.1037/pst0000356

Rossberg, J. I., Karterud, S., Pedersen, G., & Friis, S. (2007). An empirical study of countertransference reactions toward patients with personality disorders. *Comprehensive Psychiatry, 48*(3), 225–30. https://doi.org/10.1016/j.comppsych.2007.02.002

Rousmaniere, T. (2016). *Deliberate practice for psychotherapists: A guide to improving clinical effectiveness.* Routledge.

Tishby, O., & Wiseman, H. (2022). Countertransference types and their relation to rupture and repair in the alliance. *Psychotherapy Research, 32*(1), 16–31.

Westerling, T. W. III, Drinkwater, R., Laws, H., Stevens, H., Ortega, S., Goodman, D., Beinashowitz, J., & Drill, R. L. (2019). Patient attachment and therapist countertransference in psychodynamic psychotherapy. *Psychoanalytic Psychology, 36*(1), 73–81. https://doi.org/10.1037/pap0000215

Winnicott, D. W. (1947). *Hate in the countertransference.* Tavistock.

Chapter 6

Therapeutic Alliance in Psychodynamic Psychotherapy

Definitions

Contemporary psychotherapy research places great significance on the therapeutic alliance. It has been identified as one of the most robust predictors of positive therapeutic outcomes. The most recent meta-analysis by Flückiger et al. (2018) on the alliance–outcome relation draws from 295 independent studies encompassing over 30,000 patients and reveals a **medium**-sized positive effect of the therapeutic alliance on treatment outcomes. Wampold (2015) estimated that there are nearly 50% more outcome research studies on treatment differences (e.g., symptom change in psychodynamic vs. cognitive-behavioral therapy) than there are studies on the alliance but that the alliance has a relation to outcome that is nearly three times greater.

The therapeutic alliance is a transtheoretical concept or common factor present in all types of therapies. Researchers commonly adopt Bordin's (1979) tripartite model of the alliance. The first aspect is the affective bond shared between the therapist and the patient, with a strong alliance characterized by a positive, friendly, and cooperative relationship. The remaining two aspects are the collaborative process of reaching and maintaining agreement on the goals and tasks of therapy. Intuitively these three dimensions are distinguishable but when researched are rarely found apart from one another (Tryon et al., 2007), suggesting alliance is a unified construct in the minds of therapists and clients.

Not all models of the alliance are this reductionistic, however. The Intersubjective Self Psychology (Hagman et al., 2019) emphasizes the importance of instances in therapy where the therapist's empathetic listening fosters a relationship that meets the narcissistic needs of the

DOI: 10.4324/9781003323167-9

patient (e.g., mirroring, an idealized other, or perceived similarity in the other), or stable self-object transference. These seemingly "quiet" times of therapeutic alliance, or *leading edge transference*, actively contribute to positive outcomes by making the patient's self stronger and more cohesive during this period. While psychotherapy researchers have been slow to discover this concept, some intensive verbatim discourse analysis confirms a process of therapist and client change within the alliance (Brier & Ornstein, 2020).

Measurement

The alliance is typically assessed using short and easy-to-complete self-report questionnaires administered at the end of therapy sessions. Perhaps the most popular is the *Working Alliance Inventory* (Horvath & Greenberg, 1989), which produces subscale scores for the three dimensions in the Bordin model. Items include "My relationship with _____ is very important to me" and "_____ and I agree about the things I will need to do in therapy to help improve my situation." The *California Psychotherapy Alliance Scales* (Gaston et al., 1998) parcel alliance into patients' capacity to form a relationship, level of commitment, emotional connection, and working consensus with their therapist, creating a four-factor representation of the alliance. The *Helping Alliance Questionnaire* (Luborsky et al., 1996) assesses alliance as perceptions of cooperation and helpfulness within the relationship. The *Session Rating Scale* (Miller et al., 2015) is an ultra-brief measure of alliance that uses a sliding scale for respondents to rate the quality of the relationship overall and on goals, tasks, and bond. Many of these alliance scales have been adapted for process groups and for the relationship between supervisee and supervisor.

From its inception, alliance research has always considered the role of perspective in measurement. Corresponding patient, therapist, and observer versions exist for nearly all alliance measures. Different relations to process can be seen with the differing perspectives, in addition to the detection of alliance ruptures (see Chapter 7). Patients consistently score higher than their therapists measuring the same session (Tryon et al., 2007). This difference may be due to therapists undervaluing the impact of their work with clients, having finer distinctions of alliance from experiences with multiple clients, or patients experiencing gratitude or specialness in their therapeutic relationship.

Frequently patients reach a measurement *ceiling effect* in their alliance ratings where relationship quality cannot be distinguished any further because the scale is at its highest. Some have advocated for therapy alliance scales that assume a positive relationship and ask about missteps or disconnections so that more variance between relationships can be seen. The *Problematic Impressions of Therapy Scale* inquires whether the therapist did things like "forgot something important that I told him/her" or "said something I could not understand" and how much these actions troubled the client (San Francisco Psychotherapy Process Group, 2022).

Significance

Typically, the alliance is measured about the third week of treatment in psychotherapy research, and this methodological choice is for practical reasons. Most symptom change happens early in the therapy, and so Session 3 allows us time to see improvement. More patients will drop out as therapy progresses, and so a larger sample size is possible when alliance is assessed sooner. Alliance early in the therapy is associated with symptom change, but the therapeutic relationship measured closer to termination is an even stronger predictor (Flückiger et al., 2018). When alliance is measured after each session and its trajectory over treatment examined, several profiles are typically found: high and steady, improving, decreasing then improving (U-shaped), and deteriorating (Eubanks et al., 2018; Kivlighan & Shaughnessy, 2000). Strong stable alliances or alliances that ultimately improve predict more symptom change, suggesting the ability to build (or repair) relationships is a therapeutic event or skill. Often monitoring systems like those for outcome plot expected trajectories of alliance for patients and inform clinicians to examine the process when the alliance is outside what is normally seen in therapy.

Patients bring qualities to therapy that contribute to the alliance like their history of helping relationships, their interpersonal difficulties, and their expectations about the therapist (Dinger et al., 2007). An intriguing notion that follows from this is that the therapeutic alliance exists even before the formal commencement of treatment, encompassing expectations regarding the therapist's helpfulness (Zilcha-Mano et al., 2014) and minimal initial contact with professionals (Hilsenroth et al., 2004). Zilcha-Mano and colleagues (2014) estimated that patients' representations of others before they even met their therapists could explain up to half of alliance scores that resulted during the therapy.

Therapists foster alliance through supportive or relational techniques (Chapter 9). Indeed in a recent study, Leibovich and colleagues (2019) showed that supportive techniques have their good effect on outcome in psychodynamic psychotherapy (PDT) by contributing to a better alliance. Therapists' perceptions of the alliance also influence the patient's experience of the relationship (Kivlighan et al., 2014; Zilcha-Mano et al., 2015; Zilcha-Mano et al., 2016), indicating therapists' hope or esteem for the relationship affects the client. Certain therapists excel in building stronger alliances with their clients when compared to others (Crits-Christoph et al., 2009; Del Re et al., 2012). Natural interpersonal skills, extensive relationship histories, and empathic abilities are part of self-selection among those who gravitate toward the profession of psychotherapy (Heinonen & Orlinsky, 2013; Nienhuis et al., 2018). At the same time, even experienced therapists can be taught to improve their alliances (Anderson et al., 2016; Crits-Christoph et al., 2009).

New Directions

Many models of alliance assume that the alliance is a stable, trait-like quality (i.e., the ability of a patient–therapist pairing to form an alliance is fixed and unlikely to change without an intervening event). High trait alliance on the part of the client or therapist enables therapy to progress more rapidly on average, as the dyad is more trusting, emotionally available, and accommodating of intervention. Conversely, other more relational or interpersonal theories held that the development of the relationship during treatment reflects a state-like, or dynamic and changing, quality of the alliance that can function as a therapeutic factor. The state component of the patient–therapist relationship changes, evolves, and may even deteriorate during the course of therapy in response to therapist and client behaviors and the therapeutic process. Leading alliance researcher Zilcha-Mano recognized this dual nature of the alliance and has proposed a novel model of the therapeutic relationship as having state- and trait-like qualities (Zilcha-Mano & Fisher, 2022). Client and therapist have trait-like characteristics that set the initial strength of the alliance. Relational experiences or PDT techniques bring state-related changes, such as improvements or decrements in the alliance. Events leading to alterations in the state level of alliance improve the patient's trait-level alliance-building ability, ultimately resulting in better-quality and more satisfying relationships.

Contemporary studies aim to identify which patients are most likely to benefit from the state-like or process-oriented component of the alliance. For example, in one study, Zilcha-Mano and Errázuriz (2015) found that patients with more severe pretreatment interpersonal problems with a stronger state-like alliance component derived greater benefits from PDT than patients with severe interpersonal issues but without a strong state-like alliance component. All clients with severe interpersonal problems benefited even more than patients with less severe interpersonal problems who exhibited a strong state-like alliance component. Another type of research is emerging looking at the changes in alliance within a session, or micro-process research. Here, alliance is captured every few minutes several times over the session. This approach allows us to examine in real time what factors influence the state-like alliance and how therapists and clients work within it (Markin & McCarthy, 2024).

References

Anderson, T., Crowley, M. E. J., Himawan, L., Holmberg, J. K., & Uhlin, B. D. (2016). Therapist facilitative interpersonal skills and training status: A randomized clinical trial on alliance and outcome. *Psychotherapy Research*, *26*(5), 511–529.

Bordin, E. S. (1979). The generalizability of the psychoanalytic concept of the working alliance. *Psychotherapy: Theory, Research & Practice*, *16*(3), 252–260. https://doi.org/10.1037/h0085885

Brier, R., & Ornstein, A. (2020). Tracking changes in the disruption/repair sequences: Important aspects of clinical work. *Psychoanalysis, Self and Context*, *16*(4), 371–379. https://doi.org/10.1080/24720038.2020.1849222

Crits-Christoph, P., Gallop, R., Temes, C. M., Woody, G., Ball, S. A., Martino, S., & Carroll, K. M. (2009). The alliance in motivational enhancement therapy and counseling as usual for substance use problems. *Journal of Consulting and Clinical Psychology*, *77*(6), 1125.

Del Re, A. C., Flückiger, C., Horvath, A. O., Symonds, D., & Wampold, B. E. (2012). Therapist effects in the therapeutic alliance–outcome relationship: A restricted-maximum likelihood meta-analysis. *Clinical Psychology Review*, *32*(7), 642–649.

Dinger, U., Strack, M., Leichsenring, F., & Henning, S. (2007). Influences of patients' and therapists' interpersonal problems and therapeutic alliance on outcome in psychotherapy. *Psychotherapy Research*, *17*(2), 148–159.

Eubanks, C. F., Muran, J. C., & Safran, J. D. (2018). Alliance rupture repair: A meta-analysis. *Psychotherapy*, *55*(4), 508.

Flückiger, C., Del Re, A. C., Wampold, B. E., & Horvath, A. O. (2018). The alliance in adult psychotherapy: A meta-analytic synthesis. *Psychotherapy*, *55*(4), 316.

Gaston, L., Thompson, L., Gallagher, D., Cournoyer, L.-G., & Gagnon, R. (1998). Alliance, technique, and their interactions in predicting outcome of behavioral, cognitive, and brief dynamic therapy. *Psychotherapy Research*, *8*(2), 190–209. https://psycnet.apa.org/record/1998-04139-006

Hagman, G., Paul, H., & Zimmermann, P. B. (Eds.). (2019). *Intersubjective self psychology: A primer*. Routledge.

Heinonen, E., & Orlinsky, D. E. (2013). Psychotherapists' personal identities, theoretical orientations, and professional relationships: Elective affinity and role adjustment as modes of congruence. *Psychotherapy Research*, *23*(6), 718–731.

Hilsenroth, M. J., Peters, E. J., & Ackerman, S. J. (2004). The development of therapeutic alliance during psychological assessment: Patient and therapist perspectives across treatment. *Journal of Personality Assessment*, *83*(3), 332–344.

Horvath, A. O., & Greenberg, L. S. (1989). Development and validation of the working alliance inventory. *Journal of Counseling Psychology*, *36*(2), 223.

Kivlighan Jr., D. M., Marmarosh, C. L., & Hilsenroth, M. J. (2014). Client and therapist therapeutic alliance, session evaluation, and client reliable change: A moderated actor–partner interdependence model. *Journal of Counseling Psychology*, *61*(1), 15.

Kivlighan Jr., D. M., & Shaughnessy, P. (2000). Patterns of working alliance development: A typology of client's working alliance ratings. *Journal of Counseling Psychology*, *47*(3), 362.

Leibovich, L., Front, O., McCarthy, K. S., & Zilcha-Mano, S. (2020). How do supportive techniques bring about therapeutic change: The role of therapeutic alliance as a potential mediator. *Psychotherapy*, *57*(2), 151–159. https://doi.org/10.1037/pst0000253

Luborsky, L., Barber, J. P., Siqueland, L., Johnson, S., Najavits, L. M., Frank, A., & Daley, D. (1996). The revised helping alliance questionnaire (HAq-II): Psychometric properties. *The Journal of Psychotherapy Practice and Research*, *5*(3), 260.

Markin, R. D., & McCarthy, K. S. (2024). Therapist contribution, client reflective functioning, and alliance rupture–repair: A microprocess case study of psychodynamic therapy for pregnancy after loss. *Psychotherapy Theory Research Practice Training, 61*(2). https://doi.org/10.1037/pst0000520

Miller, S. D., Hubble, M. A., Chow, D., & Seidel, J. (2015). Beyond measures and monitoring: Realizing the potential of feedback-informed treatment. *Psychotherapy*, *52*(4), 449–457.

Nienhuis, J. B., Owen, J., Valentine, J. C., Winkeljohn Black, S., Halford, T. C., Parazak, S. E., Budge, S., & Hilsenroth, M. (2018). Therapeutic alliance, empathy, and genuineness in individual adult psychotherapy: A meta-analytic review. *Psychotherapy Research*, *28*(4), 593–605.

San Francisco Process Research Group. (2022). *Problematic impressions of therapy scale*. Unpublished measure.

Tryon, G. S., Blackwell, S. C., & Hammel, E. F. (2007). A meta-analytic examination of client-therapist perspectives of the working alliance. *Psychotherapy Research, 17*(6), 629–642. https://doi.org/10.1080/10503300701320611

Wampold, B. E. (2015). How important are the common factors in psychotherapy? An update. *World Psychiatry, 14*(3), 270–277.

Zilcha-Mano, S., Dinger, U., McCarthy, K. S., & Barber, J. P. (2014). Does alliance predict symptoms throughout treatment, or is it the other way around? *Journal of Consulting and Clinical Psychology, 82*(6), 931.

Zilcha-Mano, S., & Errázuriz, P. (2015). One size does not fit all: Examining heterogeneity and identifying moderators of the alliance–outcome association. *Journal of Counseling Psychology, 62*(4), 579.

Zilcha-Mano, S., & Fisher, H. (2022). Distinct roles of state-like and trait-like patient–therapist alliance in psychotherapy. *Nature Reviews Psychology, 1*, 194–210.

Zilcha-Mano, S., Muran, J. C., Hungr, C., Eubanks, C. F., Safran, J. D., & Winston, A. (2016). The relationship between alliance and outcome: Analysis of a two-person perspective on alliance and session outcome. *Journal of Consulting and Clinical Psychology, 84*(6), 484.

Zilcha-Mano, S., Solomonov, N., Chui, H., McCarthy, K. S., Barrett, M. S., & Barber, J. P. (2015). Therapist-reported alliance: Is it really a predictor of outcome? *Journal of Counseling Psychology, 62*(4), 568.

Chapter 7

Alliance Rupture and Repair in Psychodynamic Psychotherapy

Definitions

An *alliance rupture* is any deterioration in the relationship, from a major breakdown to a minor tension or a misunderstanding between the therapist and client (Eubanks et al., 2018, 2023). A rupture could be a loud confrontation, a silent impasse, a subtle moment of inattentiveness, or an inability to attune to one another. Alliance ruptures either are an expression of confrontation on the part of the client or therapist or an effort to withdraw from the relationship through distancing or overcompliance, as depicted in Table 7.1. *Rupture repair* or *resolution* is when the alliance is restored by the therapist and client working together to correct and learn from the initiating problem. Different types of ruptures require different strategies for repair.

Investigation of this subject is a shining example of how psychodynamic theory and practice can guide research, and empirical investigation can meaningfully inform practice and support theory. Alliance rupture-resolution research is embedded in a relational-intersubjective framework in which the actions of both therapist and client, rather than just the patient's pathology, contribute to the strains within the therapeutic alliance as well as to its strengthening (Eubanks et al., 2018; 2023). Sequences of in-session processes for successful rupture resolution were mapped using *task analysis*, a qualitative research technique. A marker (here, a rupture) is first identified in a session. Then, events preceding and following the marker are coded and examined for patterns in cases that achieved good or poor outcome. In successful rupture repairs, the dyad joins in noticing and disengaging the rupture, exploring the experience in the here-and-now, and expressing vulnerability. From negotiating the dynamics of their relationship, the therapist and

DOI: 10.4324/9781003323167-10

Table 7.1 Types of Alliance Ruptures

Type	Movement	In-Session Description	Resolution
Confrontation	Against	Discomfort in relationship Expression of dissatisfaction Passive-aggression	Easy to detect Often needs immediate response Correct or apologize for precipitating action Anger acknowledged as secondary to vulnerable emotion
Withdrawal	Away	Speech is quieter, much less Emotional distance or coldness Inattention or distraction Does not attend session	Sometimes harder to detect Requires reengagement in alliance Acknowledgement of anger, sadness, disappointment, or fear
	Toward	Conforming Overly agreeable Not challenging Reinforcing to client and therapist	Hardest to detect Action as secondary to vulnerable emotion Recognize as defense to anger, fear, and disappointment

client become mindful of their own internal states and how their outward behavior is congruent or prevents them from providing for each other's needs (Eubanks et al., 2018). Many times alliance ruptures are transference–countertransference enactments that can be transformed into new opportunities for insight and growth. Unskillfully managed ruptures can lead to dissatisfaction in the relationship, reinforcement of enactment patterns, and premature termination (Chapter 13).

Elaborating the alliance rupture-resolution sequence, Eubanks and colleagues (2023) encouraged therapists to prioritize the therapeutic relationship by actively observing how patients might avoid communicating experiences of anger toward the therapist, feelings of sadness and vulnerability, or needs for agency and self-assertion. Therapists' openness to the influence of their own behaviors and attitudes is also critical, as these might elicit ruptures or impair their repair. Optimal repair centers on addressing patients' underlying fears and needs within the therapeutic relationship and in their broader interpersonal connections outside therapy. According to this perspective, psychotherapists seeking to recognize and repair ruptures effectively should cultivate three interdependent therapist meta-communication skills: self-awareness, affect regulation, and interpersonal sensitivity (Eubanks et al., 2023). Metacommunication encourages collaboration between therapists and patients, fostering curiosity about what is transpiring between them. While metacommunication may involve drawing connections between the patient–therapist interaction and other relationships, the primary focus should remain on the therapeutic relationship and the present moment.

It should be recognized that the profundity of patients' disappointments within the therapeutic relationship as a curative factor was originally introduced even before relational and intersubjective approaches by Heinz Kohut, the founder of Self Psychology. Empathic failures refer to moments in therapy when therapists struggle to maintain their empathetic stance, resulting in patients experiencing disappointment and a breakdown in the previously established therapeutic rapport. These therapist failures trigger real feelings, behaviors, and memories in patients resembling similar disappointments in earlier relationships. Kohut emphasized the importance of taking these disappointments seriously at face value, rather than viewing them as defenses or resistance to therapy. Instead, they can be chances to explore through empathy aspects of the self that had previously been dissociated and now surface in therapy. While Kohut's concepts, like many other psychoanalytic ideas, have been demonstrated through numerous case studies and examples, sadly they have not been the consistent subject of empirical research.

Measurement

Ruptures can be assessed through self-report questionnaires administered after therapy sessions. The *Post-Session Questionnaire* has three items that measure the presence of any ruptures, the degree of tension in the session, and its resolution (Eubanks et al., 2018). Outside observers can analyze session recordings or transcripts for specific wordings, reactions, or processes in a session (Colli & Lingiardi, 2009; Eubanks et al., 2019). An extremely novel method has been to distinguish rupture events by examining client and therapist vocal patterns in the session (Dolev-Amit et al., 2022). Over a treatment, sessions with a rupture can be detected by fluctuations or statistical deviations in an individual patient's alliance scores given every session (Stiles et al., 2004). Each method has its advantages (e.g., privileged knowledge from the client's feelings; observation of behavior unconscious to the therapist and patient) and produces different frequencies of rupture occurrences. Therapists rate ruptures in the therapeutic alliance to be rare but observers of therapy sessions tend to rate almost every session as having at least one rupture, indicating alliance setbacks may go unnoticed or unacknowledged (Safran et al., 2011). Clients are the least likely to report alliance ruptures, perhaps being more protective or gracious when describing their relationships with their therapists (Safran et al., 2011).

Significance

Research has shown that the deliberate repair of ruptures contributes to better outcomes, particularly when undertaken intentionally by the therapist and client (as opposed to indirect or spontaneous resolution). A meta-analysis, led by Catherine Eubanks et al. (2018), drew from 11 studies involving a sample of 1,314 patients to demonstrate that rupture repair is associated with improved outcomes with a **medium**-sized effect. This improvement was observed when comparing the outcomes of patients who experienced rupture repair episodes to those who did not experience any ruptures at all or to those whose ruptures remained unrepaired. Importantly, the studies included in this meta-analysis were not limited to psychodynamic psychotherapy (PDT), indicating that the repair of ruptures is a common factor across different types of therapies. Nevertheless, as in the context of alliance research, PDT holds particular significance in understanding the dynamics of ruptures and repairs.

In qualitative interviews conducted with patients about their post-therapy memories of ruptures and repairs, patients whose ruptures were successfully resolved with the therapist's help reported a better treatment process and outcome than patients whose ruptures were not successfully resolved (Ben David-Sela, 2024). The study revealed three themes of ruptures and four themes of repairs. The most frequent rupture theme involved a disagreement on treatment tasks. The second theme was a strain in the emotional bond with the therapist, including difficulties in opening up and connecting, feeling dismissed, and a lack of attunement. The third theme was discomfort with the therapy's setting. Patients appreciated when their therapists changed the treatment tasks, helped them explore the rupture, validated their experience, and apologized to them.

Research shows the primary focus should remain on the therapeutic relationship and the present moment for rupture repair. The therapist should not rush to intervene and should remain open and non-defensive. Therapist immediacy or presence in the here-and-now promotes the detection and resolution of rupture (Hill et al., 2013). Psychoanalytic tendency has been to interpret the rupture as a resistance and connect the event back to interpersonal patterns (often the ultimate goal of rupture-resolution work), but the therapist needs to attend to the relationship first. Technique use can be deleterious in the wake of a rupture before it is understood and experienced (Gerostathos et al., 2014). Many times intervention may be the reason for the rupture! Research suggests that making such connections is more effective when done in a different session after the initial rupture has been resolved (Gerostathos et al., 2014).

When alliance ruptures are recognized and addressed, they can become meaningful therapeutic events. Conversely, if left unaddressed, they can hinder the therapeutic process (Chen et al., 2018). When looking for connections between countertransference and ruptures, negative countertransference patterns were associated with more ruptures and less resolution (Tishby & Wiseman, 2022). Positive patterns predicted resolution when the therapists' countertransference patterns were similar to positive patterns with parents. When therapists who held positive countertransference patterns toward their patients tried to repair negative patterns patients had with their parents, those efforts actually predicted ruptures and not repairs.

New Directions

This emphasis on rupture and repair research led to the development of Brief Relational Therapy (BRT) and a specific supervision process known as Alliance-Focused Training (Muran et al., 2005). On top of taking a PDT framework, BRT places a strong emphasis on recognizing and repairing ruptures to the relationship. In a study comparing PDT, cognitive-behavioral therapy (CBT), and BRT, the three treatments showed equivalent outcomes but BRT had fewer patients who dropped out. What was interesting about this study was clients who did not improve after one therapy crossed over to another treatment (e.g., someone not benefiting from CBT might receive a course of BRT). BRT had comparatively better outcomes for nonresponders in the second phase than did PDT or CBT treatment (Muran et al., 2005). The strategies for alliance rupture resolution in BRT may sometimes lead to more ruptures (Eubanks et al., 2019). These strategies are based on the abilities and motivation of both patients and therapists to frequently discuss their relationship. As a result, they may not be suitable for every patient–therapist pair or every therapeutic situation.

During the COVID lockdowns, Dolev-Amit and colleagues (2021) proposed a model for addressing withdrawal ruptures in remote therapy indirectly by using supportive techniques. Research on this model has shown that rupture resolutions occurring in a therapeutic environment characterized by a strong attachment to the therapist, a good alliance, and involving more common factors techniques tended to lead to better resolutions (Ben David-Sela et al., 2021). While this model has been clinically demonstrated, it has not yet been empirically examined.

References

Ben David-Sela, T., Dolev-Amit, T., Eubanks, C. F., & Zilcha-Mano, S. (2021). Achieving successful resolution of alliance ruptures: For whom and when? *Psychotherapy Research, 31*(7), 870–881.

Ben David-Sela, T., Leibovich, L., Khoury, Y., Hill, C. E., & Zilcha-Mano, S. (2024). "Picking up the pieces": Patients' retrospective reflections of rupture resolution episodes during treatment. *Psychotherapy Research, 34*(7), 858–871. https://doi.org/10.1080/10503307.2023.2245128

Chen, R., Atzil-Slonim, D., Bar-Kalifa, E., Hasson-Ohayon, I., & Refaeli, E. (2018). Therapists' recognition of alliance ruptures as a moderator of change in alliance and symptoms. *Psychotherapy Research, 28*(4), 560–570.

Colli, A., & Lingiardi, V. (2009). The collaborative interactions scale: A new transcript-based method for the assessment of therapeutic alliance ruptures and resolutions in psychotherapy. *Psychotherapy Research, 19*(6), 718–734. https://doi.org/10.1080/10503300903121098

Dolev-Amit, T., Leibovich, L., & Zilcha-Mano, S. (2023). Repairing alliance ruptures using supportive techniques in telepsychotherapy during the COVID-19 pandemic. In *How the COVID-19 pandemic transformed the mental health landscape* (pp. 96–109). Routledge.

Dolev-Amit, T., Nof, A., Asaad, A., Tchizick, A., & Zilcha-Mano, S. (2022). The melody of ruptures: Identifying ruptures through acoustic markers. *Counselling Psychology Quarterly, 35*(4), 724–743. https://doi.org/10.1080/09515070.2020.1860906

Eubanks, C. F., Lubitz, J., Muran, J. C., & Safran, J. D. (2019). Rupture resolution rating system (3RS): Development and validation. *Psychotherapy Research, 29*(3), 306–319. https://doi.org/10.1080/10503307.2018.1552034

Eubanks, C. F., Muran, J. C., & Safran, J. D. (2018). Alliance rupture repair: A meta-analysis. *Psychotherapy, 55*(4), 508.

Eubanks, C. F., Samstag, L. W., & Muran, J. C. (2023). *Rupture and repair in psychotherapy: A critical process for change*. American Psychological Association. https://doi.org/10.1037/0000306-000

Gerostathos, A., de Roten, Y., Berney, S., Despland, J. N., & Ambresin, G. (2014). How does addressing patient's defenses help to repair alliance ruptures in psychodynamic psychotherapy? An exploratory study. *The Journal of Nervous and Mental Disease, 202*(5), 419–424.

Hill, C. E., Gelso, C. J., Chui, H., Spangler, P. T., Hummel, A., Huang, T., Jackson, J., Jones, R. A., Palma, B., Bhatia, A., Gupta, S., Ain, S. C., Klingaman, B., Lim, R. H., Liu, J., Hui, K., Jezzi, M. M., & Miles, J. R. (2013). To be or not to be immediate with clients: The use and perceived effects of immediacy in psychodynamic/interpersonal psychotherapy. *Psychotherapy Research, 24*(3), 299–315. https://doi.org/10.1080/10503307.2013.812262

Muran, J. C., Safran, J. D., Samstag, L. W., & Winston, A. (2005). Evaluating an alliance-focused treatment for personality disorders. *Psychotherapy: Theory, Research, Practice, Training, 42*(4), 532.

Safran, J. D., Muran, J. C., & Eubanks-Carter, C. (2011). Repairing alliance ruptures. *Psychotherapy, 48*(1), 80.

Stiles, W. B., Glick, M. J., Osatuke, K., Hardy, G. E., Shapiro, D. A., Agnew-Davies, R., & Barkham, M. (2004). Patterns of alliance development and the rupture-repair hypothesis: Are productive relationships U-shaped or V-shaped? *Journal of Counseling Psychology, 51*(1), 81.

Tishby, O., & Wiseman, H. (2022). Countertransference types and their relation to rupture and repair in the alliance. *Psychotherapy Research, 32*(1), 16–31.

Chapter 8

Real Relationship in Psychodynamic Psychotherapy

Definitions

The shift from a one-person model of psychotherapy to a two-person model has brought into focus the presence of the therapist in the therapeutic relationship. The therapist is not just a blank screen for patients' projections or an instrument to detect patients' problems but an actual contributor to the relationship who brings parts of their self to therapy. This additional element of the therapeutic relationship, the real relationship (RR), is the authentic connection that the client and therapist share (Gelso et al., 2018). It goes beyond the therapeutic alliance in that it does not exist for the purpose of therapeutic work, but is a co-constructed experience felt on a more personal, less analytical, level. Greenson (1967) established the RR as "transference-free" consisting of two elements: *genuineness* and *realism*. Genuineness can be experienced as spontaneity, authenticity, and willingness to reveal the true self. Realism is the connection between two complex and imperfect human beings and the perception of the other for who they truly are, as opposed to how one wishes them to be. While RR is often positive, it reflects the whole person including uncomfortable and unlikeable parts. Clients and therapists can genuinely disappoint or anger one another or could be realistically scared for the well-being of the other at some point in the therapy.

RR grows and evolves and so has magnitude or level (Gelso et al., 2012; Lee & Choi, 2019). A high magnitude of RR with the therapist would lead to a positive restorative relationship, whereas a low level of RR could be a relationship full of transference and countertransference or be transactional with rigid professional roles. Indeed, transference may be the opposite of RR. Psychotherapy proceeds through cultivation and analysis of the transference, and in a successful therapy,

DOI: 10.4324/9781003323167-11

it is the RR that replaces transference. The patient is able to see the therapist for who they are and what they have done together, and the therapist is able to be real and genuine in that relationship. The RR provides a reciprocally meaningful relationship experience that can ideally generalize to other interpersonal contacts in the client's life. With a forming RR, the therapist can dare to be honest with the client and use their own experiences of the client to promote insightful and deeper discussion. The qualities of genuineness and realness allow for greater trust and deeper work within the therapeutic relationship on the interpersonal patterns of the client (Gelso et al., 2018). Further, the therapist and client can actively work to repair alliance ruptures that can occur during honest disclosure in therapy (see Chapter 7). This authentic presence has been shown to predict symptom change over and above the contribution of other factors (Gelso et al., 2018).

Measurement

RR is embedded in the communication between the client and therapist and involves a perspective that is privileged and internal to both parties. It is also what the relationship could become—the willingness to disclose or the deep feeling that can sustain the relationship. Not surprisingly, attempts at measuring RR have been mostly through self-report, like the *Real Relationship Inventory* (Kelley et al., 2010). Items were specifically written to measure realness and genuineness and not liking or working ability ("the relationship between my therapist and me was strengthened by our understanding of one another"; "my therapist seemed genuinely connected to me"). The two subscales are typically very highly correlated with one another, and to a lesser by still very high degree with alliance scores (Kelley et al., 2010). Importantly, RR can be differentiated from social desirability, which is the desire to change in order to present oneself as likable. Therapist and client versions exist and are generally correlated with one another (Kelley et al., 2010). When examined by subscale, genuineness is highly correlated in the dyad whereas realism is not, suggesting therapist and client accurately signal their congruence with one another but may have different perceptions of whether they know the other.

Recently, observers can rate a prototype describing the psychotherapy process of sessions showing high RR (Spina et al., 2024). Experts identified items that are most likely ("therapist is sensitive to the patient's feelings, attuned to the patient; empathic" and "patient is introspective, readily explores inner thoughts and feelings") and least likely ("therapist condescends to, or patronizes the patient" and "patient does not feel understood by therapist") to occur in high RR sessions. Higher degree of correspondence to the prototype also correlates with alliance ratings for the same sessions (Spina et al., 2024).

Significance

The RR exists outside the working alliance and the interpersonal patterns that clients bring to therapy. RR does have a strong correlation to the alliance (Kelley et al., 2010), although this relation is not as strong as the correlation between genuineness and realism. RR is negatively associated with attachment avoidance but not attachment anxiety (Fuertes et al., 2019; Marmarosh et al., 2009), such that when patients enter therapy more reluctant or less trusting, they develop a less strong RR with their therapists. Negative transference, rated by the therapist, was related to lower RR, indicating that transference might obscure or block RR from arising (Marmarosh et al., 2009).

The RR can be observed in treatment as early as the first session (Gelso et al., 2012; Lee & Choi, 2019). Assumedly RR exists before treatment as a capacity to share the true self, although this has never been measured. RR is also probably sensitive to events in the initial encounters and to the other in the dyad (i.e., shift or correct based on safety, trustworthiness, or disclosure). Transference and alliance, on the other hand, might accommodate disconfirmatory experience or information more readily (i.e., remain the same or explain away contradiction). RR remains stable over short periods (Kelley et al., 2010). In many dyads, it increases in magnitude over treatment (Gelso et al., 2012; Lee & Choi, 2019). Some therapists have stronger abilities to form RR than others (Kivilighan et al., 2016).

In a meta-analysis of 16 studies, RR was found to have **medium**-sized positive effects on both session quality and symptom improvement (Gelso et al., 2018). Client and therapist ratings of the RR were equally predictive. Interestingly, RR later in therapy is more predictive of outcome than it is when measured earlier, supporting the idea that RR might replace transference and symptoms. RR can be found in all therapeutic orientations (Gelso et al., 2018), but not enough data tell us whether the magnitude of RR and its relation to outcome differs among therapies.

New Directions

RR emerges as a product of its times, the postmodern and relativistic world where reality is cocreated (Gelso, 2009). In so far RR reflects acknowledgment of the whole person in a relationship; interpersonal and relational thinkers might find RR a useful description of health for a client and success in therapy. One hangup noted by Gelso (2009) is in the theoretical conceptualization of RR as a bipolar construct—at one end is the authentic, sincere relationship that client and therapist can hold together, whereas at the opposing end is failure to see the other person due to past relationship images. Relational thinkers eschew transference distortion and believe there is no static true self to know, believing that the present self-other configuration in a dyad is reality, the best construction which two people have created for that moment.

Growing up parallel with RR is the philosophy is multiculturalism, or the locating of persons and identities within contexts and historical systems. RR represents the balance of seeing the person while honoring their background and being open to what is yet to be revealed or discovered together. RR has been shown to exist in several countries (Lee & Choi, 2019; Lo Coco et al., 2011), but what RR is and how it is experienced may vary by culture. Therapists perceived by their clients as able to work in the multicultural space also held stronger RR with one another (Owen et al., 2011). RR and multicultural orientation were related to symptom change but worked by independent pathways by the end of therapy.

References

Fuertes, J. N., Moore, M., & Ganley, J. (2019). Therapists' and clients' ratings of real relationship, attachment, therapist self-disclosure, and treatment progress. *Psychotherapy Research*, *29*(5), 594–606. https://doi.org/10.1080/10 503307.2018.1425929

Gelso, C. J. (2009). The real relationship in a postmodern world: Theoretical and empirical explorations. *Psychotherapy Research*, *19*(3), 253–264. https://doi.org/10.1080/10503300802389242

Gelso, C. J., Kivlighan, D. M., Busa-Knepp, J., Spiegel, E. B., Ain, S., & Hummel, A. M., et al. (2012). The unfolding of the real relationship and the outcome of brief psychotherapy. *Journal of Counseling Psychology*, *59*, 495–506.

Gelso, C. J., Kivlighan, D. M. Jr., & Markin, R. D. (2018). The real relationship and its role in psychotherapy outcome: A meta-analysis. *Psychotherapy*, *55*(4), 434–444. https://doi.org/10.1037/pst0000183

Greenson, R. (1967). *The technique and practice of psychoanalysis (Vol. 1)*. International Universities Press.

Kelley, F. A., Gelso, C. J., Fuertes, J. N., Marmarosh, C., & Lanier, S. H. (2010). The real relationship inventory: Development and psychometric investigation of the client form. *Psychotherapy: Theory, Research, Practice, Training*, *47*(4), 540.

Kivlighan, D. M., Jr., Hill, C. E., Gelso, C. J., & Baumann, E. (2016). Working alliance, real relationship, session quality, and client improvement in psychodynamic psychotherapy: A longitudinal actor partner interdependence model. *Journal of Counseling Psychology*, *63*(2), 149–161. https://doi.org/10.1037/cou0000134

Lee, E., & Choi, H. N. (2019). The unfolding of the Korean client- and counselor-rated real relationship and the counseling outcome in Korea. *Asia Pacific Education Review*, *20*, 533–542. https://doi.org/10.1007/s12564-019-09586-0

Lo Coco, G., Gullo, S., Prestano, C., & Gelso, C. J. (2011). Relation of the real relationship and the working alliance to the outcome of brief psychotherapy. *Psychotherapy*, *48*(4), 359.

Marmarosh, C. L., Gelso, C. J., Markin, R. D., Majors, R., Mallery, C., & Choi, J. (2009). The real relationship in psychotherapy: Relationships to adult attachments, working alliance, transference, and therapy outcome. *Journal of Counseling Psychology*, *56*(3), 337–350. https://doi.org/10.1037/a0015169

Owen, J. J., Tao, K., Leach, M. M., & Rodolfa, E. (2011). Clients' perceptions of their psychotherapists' multicultural orientation. *Psychotherapy*, *48*(3), 274–282. https://doi.org/10.1037/a0022065

Spina, D. S., Aafjes-Van Doorn, K., & Békés, V. (2024). Development of a psychotherapy process prototype for the real relationship. *Psychotherapy Research*, *34*(4), 449–460. https://doi.org/10.1080/10503307.2023.2191801

Part III

Interventions

Evidence in Psychodynamic Psychotherapy: A Contemporary Introduction

Chapter 9

Supportive Techniques in Psychodynamic Psychotherapy

Definitions

Supportive interventions, in general, aim to strengthen the patient's adaptive functioning, enhance self-esteem, facilitate regulation of emotions, and encourage mature psychological defenses (Gabbard, 2017; Rasmussen & Kealy, 2020). They are thought to shore up or promote patients' psychological abilities to get internal needs met in the external world. Factors common to many treatments, like demonstrating warmth and empathy, can be considered supportive techniques, as can interventions more unique to psychodynamic therapy (PDT), like boundary setting, emotion identification, and bolstering adaptive defenses (Markowitz, 2014). The exact delineation of supportive techniques is hazy because they were first defined by negation as any interventions not psychoanalytic and therefore appropriate for use with the unanalyzable (Markowitz, 2014; Rasmussen & Kealy, 2020). As clinicians and theorists expanded psychoanalysis to treat more impairing conditions, many supportive interventions like demonstrating empathy came to be recognized for their psychoanalytic usefulness and their creation of a therapy atmosphere that enables further exploration and depth work.

What has presumed to be supported are the ego functions and defenses (i.e., essential mental activities like perception, judgment, frustration tolerance, and psychological mindedness; Gabbard, 2017). Therapists focus the patient's attention away from distressing or confusing experiences toward the relevant or rational elements in a situation. They encourage logical problem-solving and work-enhancing strategies and promote positive experiences and emotions with the patient. Table 9.1 lists four basic types of supportive interventions. These techniques vary in the level of support provided, the use of the

DOI: 10.4324/9781003323167-13

Table 9.1 Dimensions of Supportive Interventions

Dimension	Exploration Elaboration Identification	Empathic Validation	Advice Praise	Suggestion Gratification Ego-Lending
Definition	Encouraging patient to provide more material	Using therapist for patient to become more aware, feel understood	Providing indirect action and reinforcement of solutions	Promoting direct action, use of therapist, and satisfaction of wishes
Responsibility	Some therapist, some client	Some more therapist and some client	Mostly therapist, some client	Very much therapist
Function	Collecting data, potential to expose conflict	Collecting data and guiding experience	Support client solutions and remove attention from unconscious conflict	Solve and cover over conflict

Note. Adapted from Gabbard (2017).

therapist, and degree of exposure or resolution of unconscious conflict. From a psychodynamic point of view (Rockland, 2003), supportive interventions are not delivered haphazardly or in a blanket fashion but in response to the therapist's formulation of the patient and the need for support in the situation (immediate level of client functioning and necessity of problem-solving). A PDT therapist does not praise the patient's actions for the mere sake of making them feel better, but because the patient specifically is not able to manage their self-esteem in a moment that they need it for functioning. Supportive interventions can be given singly or can be delivered as part of a supportive psychotherapy treatment package, several of which have been fashioned.

Supportive therapy is especially helpful for lower functioning persons or those in crisis acutely lacking skills to manage their internal and external environments. Persons with healthy ego function and defenses are thought to benefit less from support, despite evidence to the contrary as we will see (Høglend et al., 2011; Zilcha-Mano et al., 2021). Less clinical and research attention has been given to supportive therapy due to the greater theoretical emphasis placed on transference work in PDT, the muted ability to see change in persons with complex problems, and the additional risk incurred with less stable patients (Markowitz, 2014; Rasmussen & Kealy, 2020). The unfortunate reality is that supportive therapy in research is commonly relegated to be a control condition and that lower functioning patients are screened out of participation.

Measurement

Assessment of supportive interventions can be a challenge due to lack of definitions, focus on outcome of the intervention instead of its function (e.g., alliance building), and overlap with many normative relational behaviors. Supportive psychodynamic interventions have been measured individually by classifying verbal statements in session transcripts (Banon et al., 2012; Connolly et al., 1998). For example, the *Verbal Response Category System* (Hill, 1978) classifies behaviors by intervention type such as minimal encourager, approval-reassurance, structuring, information, and advice. These measures yield frequency counts of the number of times a supportive technique is employed or percentages of supportive interventions relative to other types of intervention categories.

Global observations of session recordings or judgments about amounts of supportive technique over the entire session are also used. The degree that supportive techniques are isolated from other types of interventions and behaviors in these instruments varies. Some measures are more psychodynamic in their description of supportive interventions (Ogrodniczuk & Piper, 1999) and others separate out general interpersonal skills ("my therapist waited for some time before giving a response"; Barber et al., 1996), whereas others include case management activities like symptom assessment and suicide prevention planning (Kolla et al., 2009). In still other measures therapists estimate the proportion of interventions that they use relative to others in a session (Bush & Meehan, 2011; Hendriksen et al., 2011).

Significance

Despite the relative lack of research and clinical attention, supportive interventions constitute much of what PDT is. Around 85–90% of the statements a therapist makes in a session are judged to be supportive in nature (with 10–15% on average classified as expressive; Banon et al., 2013; Connolly et al., 1998). Use of supportive technique is lower in psychoanalysis but still is the majority of the interventions that the therapist provided (Banon et al., 2013; Bush & Meehan, 2011). Purely supportive PDT can be readily distinguished in its levels of supportive techniques from PDT that includes an expressive component (Barber et al., 1996; Connolly et al., 1998; Ogrodniczuk & Piper, 1999; Zilcha-Mano et al., 2021). Cognitive-behavioral treatments, which tend to have higher therapist activity levels than PDT, show higher proportions of supportive interventions than do PDT treatments (Banon et al., 2013), although many cognitive-behavioral interventions can be categorized as supportive. Over treatment, the levels of supportive techniques used remained constant (Kolla et al., 2009) or declined (Banon et al., 2013). Therapists were more likely to use supportive interventions when they also felt positive or protective countertransference toward their patients (Colli et al., 2022). Within sessions, PDT therapists used a consistent, high level of support, but these interventions tended to become more structured toward the end of the sessions (Hill, 1978).

Supportive techniques have a robust relation to the strength of the alliance. When therapists deliver more supportive interventions in PDT, they also evidence stronger alliances (Ogrodniczuk & Piper, 1999). No studies have been conducted on whether supportive interventions change ego function levels, but there is evidence for their effect on increasing adaptive defense use (Colli et al., 2022). Surprisingly, there has consistently been no result when levels of supportive interventions were correlated with symptom outcomes (Barber et al., 1996; Ogrodniczuk & Piper, 1999). This finding is probably because everyone benefits from supportive techniques, and more interventions are likely to be given to persons who may not show much improvement. However, well-implemented supportive psychotherapies generally are as effective at symptom reduction as other treatments, even for chronic or characterological disorders (Cuijpers et al., 2024).

New Directions

Leibovich and colleagues (2018) reconceptualized supportive interventions as interpersonal in nature, bringing about a corrective emotional experience in the therapy relationship. Instead of working through increasing the patients' ego functioning, supportive interventions might be a relational opportunity for help and connection, which leads to a new experience for the patient and the development of the therapeutic alliance. The therapist attempts to deeply understand the client and deeply experience the relationship while stepping out of repeated enactments ("choosing 'acts of freedom'," p. 235) to facilitate a new relational experience of being helped.

In this model, the therapist first assesses the patient's most central unmet need, which may be latent or not expressed directly. The therapist then examines their own reaction to the patient, the response of other, and how this lines up with the therapeutic situation. Then through empathy the therapist understands how the patient is experiencing their encounter together, relative to the therapists' formulation. On many occasions, this may be sufficient, given that it should provide a new understanding of the patient and the therapeutic process. Sometimes the therapist would need to step out of the enactment by choosing a new behavior that better fits this new understanding of the patient. Leibovich et al. (2018, 2020) demonstrated this interpersonal process in both empirical and case study methods. In case studies, the important or missing element was identified as choosing "acts of freedom" not to repeat the patient's interpersonal pattern. In empirical work, the correlation between the amount of supportive interventions used in a session to the amount of symptom improvement over therapy could be fully explained through the development of a better alliance, meaning supportive techniques built alliance which then changed symptoms.

References

Banon, E., Perry, J. C., Semeniuk, T., Bond, M., de Roten, Y., Hersoug, A. G., & Despland, J.-N. (2013). Therapist interventions using the psychodynamic interventions rating scale in dynamic therapy, psychoanalysis, and CBT. *Psychotherapy Research*, *23*(2), 121–136. https://doi.org/10.1080/10503307.2012.745955

Barber, J. P., Crits-Christoph, P., & Luborsky, L. (1996). Effects of therapist adherence and competence on patient outcome in brief dynamic therapy. *Journal of Consulting and Clinical Psychology*, *64*(3), 619.

Bush, M., & Meehan, W. (2011). Should supportive measures and relational variables be considered a part of psychoanalytic technique? Some empirical considerations. *International Journal of Psychoanalysis*, *92*(2), 377–399. https://doi.org/10.1111/j.1745-8315.2011.00403.x

Colli, A., Gagliardini, G., & Gullo, S. (2022). Countertransference responses mediate the relationship between patients' overall defense functioning and therapists' interventions. *Psychotherapy Research*, *32*(1), 32–45. https://doi.org/10.1080/10503307.2021.1884768

Connolly, M. B., Crits-Christoph, P., Shappell, S., Barber, J. P., & Luborsky, L. (1998). Therapist interventions in early sessions of brief supportive-expressive psychotherapy for depression. *Journal of Psychotherapy Practice and Research*, *7*(4), 290.

Cuijpers, P., Miguel, C., Ciharova, M., Harrer, M., & Karyotaki, E. (2024). Nondirective supportive therapy for depression: A meta-analytic review. *Journal of Affective Disorders*, *349*, 452–461. https://doi.org/10.1016/j.jad.2024.01.073

Gabbard, G. O. (2017). *Long-term psychodynamic psychotherapy: A basic text* (3rd ed.). American Psychiatric Association Publishing.

Hendriksen, M., Van, H. L., Schoevers, R. A., De Jonghe, F. E., Van Wijk, C. M. G., Peen, J., & Dekker, J. J. (2011). Therapist judgment of defense styles and therapeutic technique related to outcome in psychodynamic psychotherapy for depression. *Psychotherapy and Psychosomatics*, *80*(6), 377–379. https://doi.org/10.1159/000324365

Hill, C. E. (1978). Development of a counselor verbal response category. *Journal of Counseling Psychology*, *25*(5), 461.

Høglend, P., Hersoug, A. G., Bøgwald, K.-P., Amlo, S., Marble, A., Sørbye, Ø., Røssberg, J. I., Ulberg, R., Gabbard, G. O., & Crits-Christoph, P. (2011). Effects of transference work in the context of therapeutic alliance and quality of object relations. *Journal of Consulting and Clinical Psychology*, *79*(5), 697–706. https://doi.org/10.1037/a0025413

Kolla, N. J., Links, P. S., McMain, S., Streiner, D. L., Cardish, R., & Cook, M. (2009). Demonstrating adherence to guidelines for the treatment of patients with borderline personality disorder. *The Canadian Journal of Psychiatry*, *54*(3), 165–175.

Leibovich, L., McCarthy, K. S., & Zilcha-Mano, S. (2020). How do supportive techniques bring about therapeutic change: The role of therapeutic alliance as a potential mediator. *Psychotherapy*, *57*(2), 151–159. https://doi.org/10.1037/pst0000232

Leibovich, L., Nof, A., Auerbach-Barber, S., & Zilcha-Mano, S. (2018). A practical clinical suggestion for strengthening the alliance based on a supportive–expressive framework. *Psychotherapy*, *55*(3), 231–240. https://doi.org/10.1037/pst0000156

Markowitz, J. C. (2014). What is supportive psychotherapy? *Focus*, *12*(3), 285–289.

Ogrodniczuk, J. S., & Piper, W. E. (1999). Measuring therapist technique in psychodynamic psychotherapies: Development and use of a new scale. *Journal of Psychotherapy Practice and Research*, *8*(2), 123–134.

Rasmussen, B., & Kealy, D. (2020). Reflections on supportive psychotherapy in the 21st century. *Journal of Social Work Practice*, *34*(3), 281–295. https://doi.org/10.1080/02650533.2019.1648245

Rockland, L. H. (2003). *Supportive therapy*. Basic Books.

Sharpless, B. A. (2019). *Psychodynamic therapy techniques: A guide to expressive and supportive interventions*. Oxford University Press.

Zilcha-Mano, S., Goldstein, P., Dolev-Amit, T., Ben David-Sela, T., & Barber, J. P. (2021). A randomized controlled trial for identifying the most suitable treatment for depression based on patients' attachment orientation. *Journal of Consulting and Clinical Psychology*, *89*(12), 985.

Chapter 10

Expressive Techniques in Psychodynamic Psychotherapy

Definitions

Expressive or interpretive interventions are designed to uncover or "express" the unconscious conflict behind a patient's symptoms (Gabbard, 2017; Sharpless, 2019). Table 10.1 describes four categories of these interventions, their function, and client and therapist responsibility for change. Expressive techniques turn attention inward and bring up times when the patient has not been able to successfully resolve unconscious conflict (e.g., making connections between when the patient felt an emotion in their developmental history and now again in the present). The challenge of looking inward and reevaluating participation in relational conflict creates strain within the patient and the therapeutic alliance. Benefit depends on factors like patient needs and functioning, present environmental demands, type and focus of expressive interventions, and alliance strength and therapist skill. Not every patient, nor all patients at every moment, is ready to put in the effort for expressive work, demanding a certain artfulness to the therapist's interventions that we will examine scientifically.

Measurement

Expressive intervention use can be examined at the level of the statement or therapy turn-in session transcripts or recordings. The *Verbal Response Category System* (Hill, 1978) has classifications for interpretation, confrontation, and clarification. Measures for confrontation and clarification have often been borrowed from the humanistic therapy literature, which often typifies these interventions as evocative, exploratory, or refocusing statements (Elliott et al., 2023). Other instruments

DOI: 10.4324/9781003323167-14

Table 10.1 Dimensions of Expressive Interventions

Dimension	Exploration Elaboration Identification	Clarification	Confrontation	Interpretation
Definition	Encouraging patient to provide more material	Highlighting experiencing of conscious or preconscious material	Pointing out discrepancy or inconsistency between thoughts, feelings, behaviors, and experience	Connections between past and present episode and unconscious conflict
Responsibility	Some therapist, some client	Some therapist, mostly client	Some therapist, mostly client	Some therapist, mostly client
Function	Collecting data and potential to expose conflict	Increasing poignancy	Decreasing defensive function	Insight and reorganization of experience

Note: Adapted from Gabbard (2017).

have been created with specific definitions of how verbal statements of these interventions might appear in psychodynamic therapy (PDT) (Connolly et al., 1998). Given their place in PDT theory and practice, the most granular focus has been on interpretation types. Table 10.2 displays the ways that two assessment tools break down the depth and focus of the interpretation. These instruments create frequency counts of specific techniques present in the session or the proportion of interventions relative to other interventions, and for some, the content or depth of the interventions.

When all types of expressive techniques (exploration, confrontation, clarification, and interpretation) are measured together, an overall or average level of PDT intervention use for a session is produced. Descriptions of common measures of PDT techniques are found in Table 10.2. Some of these measures attempt to describe interventions in jargon-free, nontechnical language so that clients, therapists, or observers can use the instrument to describe their view of what happened in a session. These intervention scales are for the general practice of PDT, not for a particular system or treatment package. *Adherence* scales are a subset of intervention measures used to determine whether a therapist followed a specific PDT manual to an established standard. *Competence* measures assess how well those interventions were delivered. Table 10.2 describes several example adherence/competence measures. Normally, expert judges will observe a session and rate the presence of each adherence item and the intervention's timing, accuracy, and delivery, including whether it should have been made at all. Adherence is typically measured for specific interventions individually. Competence can be assessed for the same items or as a global overall score for a session. Adherence and competence are not strongly correlated (Barber et al., 2007). Reliability for competency is typically lower than for adherence because agreeing an intervention occurred is easier than deciding that it was done effectively.

Significance

Expressive interventions make up a relatively small portion of therapist actions in the therapy relative to supportive interventions. Consistently, only 10–15% of statements the therapist makes are expressive (Banon et al., 2012; Connolly et al., 1998; Hill, 1978). Dynamic interventions are seen even in early sessions of PDT (Hill, 1978; Keefe et al., 2019; McMillen & Hilsenroth, 2019) and increase in levels over

Table 10.2 Measures of Expressive Interventions

Measure	Purpose	Output	Dimensions
		Statement-Level Ratings	
Psychodynamic Interpretation Rating Scale (Banon et al., 2012)	Defense and transference interpretations	Frequency Type Depth	Addresses defense OR affect; Addresses defense AND affect; Addresses motive, defense, AND affect Links motive linked to past
Transference Work Scale (Høglend et al., 2011)	Interpretations of the therapeutic relationship	Frequency Completeness	Any mention of therapy Thoughts and feelings about therapy Beliefs about therapist Linking therapist to conflict Linking therapist to interpersonal patterns
		Session-Level Ratings	
Psychotherapy Process Q-sort (Leichsenring et al., 2016)	Describe the most typical and least typical processes in session	Rank-order of processes	Prototypes of 20 most representative and 20 least representative processes for psychodynamic, psychoanalytic, cognitive-behavioral, relational, and interpersonal therapies
Comparative Psychotherapy Process Scale (Hilsenroth et al., 2005)	Empirically derived descriptions of psychodynamic and cognitive-behavioral techniques	Overall average scores	Subscales for psychodynamic-interpersonal and cognitive-behavioral treatments

(Continued)

Table 10.2 (Continued)

Measure	Purpose	Output	Dimensions
Multitheoretical List of Therapeutic Interventions (McCarthy & Barber, 2009)	Jargon-free, nontechnical descriptions of therapeutic actions	Overall average scores	Subscales for behavioral, cognitive, dialectical-behavioral, interpersonal, person-centered, psychodynamic, and experiential therapies and common factors
Adherence and Competence Ratings			
Penn Adherence-Competence Scales (Barber & Crits-Christoph, 1993)	Adherence and competence to supportive–expressive therapy	Overall average scores	Subscales for general therapeutic skills; supportive technique use; expressive technique use
Interactive Process Assessment (Keefe et al., 2019)	Adherence to panic-focused psychodynamic psychotherapy	Scores on therapists' focus in session	Panic dynamics focus Transference Early relationships Present relationships Ego defenses Patient exploration
Interpretive and Supportive Technique Scale (Ogrodniczuk & Piper, 1999)	Adherence to supportive-interpretive therapy	Degree of adherence	Mostly supportive to mostly expressive

therapy (Banon et al., 2012; Keefe et al., 2019; Klein et al., 2003) or remain steady (Barber & Crits-Christoph, 1996; Owen & Hilsenroth, 2014). Other psychotherapies like cognitive-behavioral therapy show significantly lower levels of expressive techniques than PDT, and conversely, PDT rarely shows a high degree of interventions from other systems (Hilsenroth et al., 2005; McCarthy & Barber, 2009).

The relation of PDT use to alliance and outcome is perplexing when there are average levels of techniques for sessions. Sometimes research shows expressive technique use is associated with improved alliance and symptom improvement but equally frequent are studies in which higher levels of expressive interventions are associated with *worse* alliances and outcomes (Barber et al., 2021). Taken together, these studies cancel one another out and show **negligible** effect in meta-analysis (Power et al., 2022). However, the finding that greater technique use has no correlation with outcome is true for every other psychotherapy as well.

When PDT interventions are examined individually, a more nuanced picture emerges, namely, that the more expressive in nature the intervention, the *less likely* the positive effect (Barber et al., 2021). Exploration of interpersonal themes and affect has a positive relation to alliance and symptom change (Diener et al., 2007); clarification and confrontation have no relation (Stiles et al., 2023); and the intervention most revealing of unconscious conflict, interpretation, is linked to *negative* outcomes (Datz et al., 2019; Ryum et al., 2010; Buchheim et al., 2023), at least in the short term. For example, Datz and colleagues (2019) observed facial expressions that occurred in sessions when different interventions were applied and saw increases in expression of contempt in both therapist and client. Wade-Bohleber and coworkers (2020) recorded patients' brainwaves during a therapeutic interview and saw brain activity increased in emotion centers and decreased in regions for sensorimotor control. Revealing unconscious or denied material or drawing direct attention to the therapy relationship has long been recognized as potentially frustrating, anxiety-provoking, shaming, or psychologically destabilizing (Strachey, 1934), experiences that which can be detrimental when not managed well. Rightfully so, Gabbard and colleagues (1994) labeled interpretation a "high risk-high gain" phenomenon.

However, PDT practitioners are also acutely aware from their work with patients of how transformative interpretive interventions can be. It is *how well* expressive techniques are delivered, and not the amount, that explains how these interventions benefit clients (Barber et al., 2021).

When the clinician is judged to be more competent in performing PDT, there is a better therapy process and more improvement, and greater competency is related to outcome in all other psychotherapies as well, albeit with a **small** effect-size (Power et al., 2022). Several factors consistently emerge in research on what makes a competent interpretation: delivery within a strong alliance, emotions in the session, accuracy to the formulation, and flexibility for the needs of the patient and therapy. Pairing interventions with moments in the therapy when the alliance is stronger is associated with better outcomes in numerous studies (Barber et al., 2021; Owen et al., 2013; Ryum et al., 2010; Keefe et al., 2019). Furthermore, expressive interventions had positive effects when they also increased the therapeutic alliance (Kivlighan et al., 2019; Patton et al., 1997). Expressive technique use with a poor alliance is almost always counter-indicated.

Dynamic interventions also have a better effect when the patient experiences emotion before and after the intervention use (Barber et al., 2021). The therapist needs to consider their own emotional state in the relationship because interpretations are less helpful when the therapist feels inadequate (Dahl et al., 2016; Nissen-Lie et al., 2022). Patients with more severe personality or attachment difficulties also may benefit more from interpretive work (Høglend et al., 2011; Keefe et al., 2019; McMillen & Hilsenroth, 2019; Zilcha-Mano et al., 2021).

Accuracy of interventions, how closely they match the patient's formulation, may be important to alliance improvement and outcome (Barber et al., 2021). Studies of accuracy capture a formulation for the patient from interviews, observations early in treatment, or therapist judgment (Crits-Christoph et al., 1988; Silberschatz, Fretter, & Curtis, 1986). They compare whether interventions match this individual formulation or not and its relation to outcome. Similarly, studies of therapists in practice found that when PDT therapists predicted their ideal interventions for a patient's formulation and were performing those interventions three months later their patients reported better outcomes (Castonguay et al., 20120).

Finally, research shows flexible use of expressive intervention use, relative to the needs of the client and situation, predicts outcome. This relation is seen when the therapist modulates the amount of expressive interventions in a session to be optimal (not too little, not too much; McCarthy et al., 2016) or across treatment (Owen & Hilsenroth, 2014). Interpretation in the middle part of PDT (the working through, Chapter 12) or later in the treatment appears to be more effective at lowering symptoms than earlier in treatment (Keefe et al., 2019; Kivlighan et al., 2019). Finally, using expressive alongside other interventions (supportive or cognitive-behavioral) may associate with more improvement (Chen et al., 2020; Owen et al., 2013) as it may connect dynamic processes with behavior change.

New Directions

Psychotherapy integration is the incorporation of therapist behaviors from multiple therapy. Advantages of psychotherapy integration are featured in Table 10.3. Most psychotherapists when asked or when their actual in-session behaviors are studied will integrate techniques (Banon et al., 2013; Orlinsky et al., 2020). Table 10.3 enumerates five ways that borrowing interventions in PDT may change psychotherapy process negatively (Busch, 2018). There are multiple methods to combine interventions, and they resolve concerns about integration in PDT to varying degrees. *Technical eclecticism* incorporates different therapeutic interventions due to problem context, patient preferences for therapy, and therapist training or experience. Techniques sit side-by-side without rationale, and their use is highly responsive to the immediate needs of the client, therapist, and therapy process. On the other hand, *theoretical integration* develops a grand theory for understanding individuals drawing from multiple domains of knowledge about the human condition. Magnavita (2006) interconnected neuroscience,

Table 10.3 Potential Advantages and Disadvantages of Psychotherapy Integration to Psychodynamic Psychotherapy

Advantages	Disadvantages
Maximize symptom improvement	Interference with insight
Shorten treatment length	Taking a side in patients' conflicts
Make more lasting change/ prevent relapse	Gratifying patients' demands
Make more accessible to less resourced persons	Incomplete resolution of symptom determinants
Connect insight to behavior change, behavior change to insight	Threat to therapeutic relationship

Note: Adapted in part from Busch (2018).

attachment, affective science, interpersonal relations, and ecological systems into a unified theory to determine when to intervene and what level to expect to see change. Such an approach has greater conceptual coherence, but the overarching theory may depart from PDT in important ways. *Assimilative integration* uses PDT as a foundation or base model and incorporates external techniques per their psychodynamic indication (e.g., the patient's early experiences inhibited their ability to learn a development skill that now should be taught by the therapist). Stricker and Gold's (1996) assimilative integrative PDT locates the patient's issue at three levels (Tier 1: behavior/interpersonal relatedness; Tier 2: cognition and emotion; Tier 3: psychodynamic conflict, object relations). Therapy proceeds at dynamic level until there is a need to switch to another level. Any time an intervention is provided from another tier, it becomes an opportunity to understand dynamically with the patient why adaptation was needed.

References

Banon, E., Perry, J. C., Semeniuk, T., Bond, M., de Roten, Y., Hersoug, A. G., & Despland, J.-N. (2012). Therapist interventions using the psychodynamic interventions rating scale in dynamic therapy, psychoanalysis, and CBT. *Psychotherapy Research*, *23*(2), 121–136. https://doi.org/10.1080/10503307.2012.745955

Barber, J. P., & Crits-Christoph, P. (1996). Development of a therapist adherence/competence rating scale for supportive-expressive dynamic psychotherapy: A preliminary report. *Psychotherapy Research*, *20*(1), 81–94. https://doi.org/10.1080/10503309612331331608

Barber, J. P., Muran, J. C., McCarthy, K. S., Keefe, J. R., & Zilcha-Mano, S. (2021). Research on dynamic therapies. In M. Barkham, W. Lutz, & L. G. Castonguay (Eds.), *Handbook of psychotherapy and behavior change* (6th ed., pp. 443–494). Wiley.

Barber, J. P., Sharpless, B. A., Klostermann, S., & McCarthy, K. S. (2007). Assessing intervention competence and its relation to therapy outcome: A selected review derived from the outcome literature. *Professional Psychology: Research and Practice*, *38*(5), 493.

Buchheim, A., Kernberg, O. F., Netzer, N., Buchheim, P., Perchtold-Stefan, C., Sperner-Unterweger, B., Beckenbauer, F., & Labek, K. (2023). Differential neural response to psychoanalytic intervention techniques during structural interviewing: A single-case analysis using EEG. *Frontiers in Human Neuroscience*, *16*, 1054518. https://doi.odg/10.3389/fnhum.2022.1054518

Busch, F. N. (2018). *Psychodynamic approaches to behavioral change*. American Psychiatric Association Publishing.

Castonguay, L. G., Janis, R. A., Youn, S. J., Xiao, H., McAleavey, A. A., Boswell, J. F., Carney, D. M., Boutselis, M. A., Braver, M., Chiswick, N. R., Hemmelstein, N. A., Jackson, J. S., Lytle, R. A., Morford, M. E., Scott, H. S., Spayd, C. S., & Wiley, M. O. (2017). Clinicians' prediction and recall of therapeutic interventions: Practice research network study, *Counselling Psychology Quarterly*, *30*(3), 308. https://doi.org/10.1080/09515070.2017.1334628

Chen, R., Rafaeli, E., Ziv-Beiman, S., Bar-Kalifa, E., Solomonov, N., Barber, J. P., Peri, T., & Atzil-Slonim, D. (2020). Therapeutic technique diversity is linked to quality of working alliance and client functioning following alliance ruptures. *Journal of Consulting and Clinical Psychology*, *88*(9), 844–858. https://doi.org/10.1037/ccp0000490

Connolly, M. B., Crits-Christoph, P., Shappell, S., Barber, J. P., & Luborsky, L. (1998). Therapist interventions in early sessions of brief supportive-expressive psychotherapy for depression. *The Journal of Psychotherapy Practice and Research*, *7*(4), 290.

Crits-Christoph, P., Cooper, A., & Luborsky, L. (1988). The accuracy of therapists' interpretations and the outcome of dynamic psychotherapy. *Journal of Consulting and Clinical Psychology*, *56*(4), 490–495. https://doi.org/10.1037/0022-006X.56.4.490

Dahl, H.-S. J., Ulberg, R., Friis, S., Perry, J. C., & Høglend, P. A. (2016). Therapists' inadequate feelings and long-term effect of transference work. *Psychotherapy and Psychosomatics*, *85*(5), 309–310. https://doi.org/10.1159/000444647

Datz, F., Wong, G., & Löffler-Stastka, H. (2019). Interpretation and working through contemptuous facial micro-expressions benefits the patient-therapist relationship. *International Journal of Environmental Research and Public Health*, *16*(24)*,* 4901. https://doi.org/10.3390/ijerph16244901

Diener, M. J., Hilsenroth, M. J., & Weinberger, J. (2007). Therapist affect focus and patient outcomes in psychodynamic psychotherapy: A meta-analysis. *American Journal of Psychiatry*, *164*(6), 936–941.

Elliott, R., Bohart, A., Larson, D., Muntigl, P., & Smoliak, O. (2023). Empathic reflections by themselves are not effective: Meta-analysis and qualitative synthesis. *Psychotherapy Research*, *33*(7), 957–973. https://doi.org/10.1080/10503307.2017.1420923

Gabbard, G. O. (2017). *Long-term psychodynamic psychotherapy: A basic text* (3rd ed.). American Psychiatric Association Publishing.

Hill, C. E. (1978). Development of a counselor verbal response category. *Journal of Counseling Psychology*, *25*(5), 461.

Hilsenroth, M. J., Blagys, M. D., Ackerman, S. J., Bonge, D. R., & Blais, M. A. (2005). Measuring psychodynamic-interpersonal and cognitive-behavioral techniques: Development of the comparative psychotherapy process scale. *Psychotherapy: Theory, Research, Practice, Training*, *42*(3), 340–356. https://doi.org/10.1037/0033-3204.42.3.340

Høglend, P., Hersoug, A. G., Bøgwald, K.-P., Amlo, S., Marble, A., Sørbye, Ø, Røssberg, J. I., Ulberg, R., Gabbard, G. O., & Crits-Christoph, P. (2011). Effects of transference work in the context of therapeutic alliance and quality of object relations. *Journal of Consulting and Clinical Psychology*, *79*(5), 697–706. https://doi.org/10.1037/a0025413

Keefe, J. R., Solomonov, N., Derubeis, R. J., Phillips, A. C., Busch, F. N., Barber, J. P., Chambless, D. L., & Milrod, B. L. (2019). Focus is key: Panic-focused interpretations are associated with symptomatic improvement in panic-focused psychodynamic psychotherapy. *Psychotherapy Research*, *29*(8), 1033–1044. https://doi.org/10.1080/10503307.2018.1464682

Kivlighan, D. M., Hill, C. E., Ross, K., Kline, K., Furhmann, A., & Sauber, E. (2019). Testing a mediation model of psychotherapy process and outcome in psychodynamic psychotherapy: Previous client distress, psychodynamic techniques, dyadic working alliance, and current client distress. *Psychotherapy Research*, *29*(5), 581–593. https://doi.org/10.1080/10503307.2017.1420923

Klein, C., Milrod, B. L., Busch, F. N., Levy, K. N., & Shapiro, T. S. (2003). A preliminary study of clinical process in relation to outcome in psychodynamic psychotherapy for panic disorder. *Psychotherapy*. https://doi.org/ 10.1037/pst0000175

Leichsenring, F., Ablon, S., Barber, J. P., Beutel, M., Gibbons, M. B. C., Crits-Christoph, P., & Salzer, S. (2016). Developing a prototype for short-term psychodynamic (supportive-expressive) therapy: An empirical study with the psychotherapy process q-set. *Psychotherapy Research*, *26*(4), 500–510.

Magnavita, J. J. (2006). In search of the unifying principles of psychotherapy: Conceptual, empirical, and clinical convergence. *American Psychologist*, *61*(8), 882–892. https://doi.org/10.1037/0003-066X.61.8.882

McCarthy, K. S., & Barber, J. P. (2009). The multitheoretical list of therapeutic interventions: Initial report. *Psychotherapy Research*, *19*(1), 96–113. https:// doi.org/10.1080/10503300802524343

McCarthy, K. S., Keefe, J. R., & Barber, J. P. (2016). Goldilocks on the couch: Moderate levels of psychodynamic and process-experiential technique predict outcome in psychodynamic therapy. *Psychotherapy Research*, *26*(3), 307–317. https://doi.org/10.1080/10503307.2014.973921

McMillen, K., & Hilsenroth, M. J. (2019). What interpersonal problems are related to different therapeutic techniques early in treatment? *Clinical Psychology & Psychotherapy*, *26*(4), 502–509. https://doi.org/10.1002/ cpp.2370

Nissen-Lie, H. A., Dahl, H. S. J., & Høglend, P. A. (2020). Patient factors predict therapists' emotional countertransference differently depending on whether therapists use transference work in psychodynamic therapy. *Psychotherapy Research*, *32*(1), 3–15. https://doi.org/10.1080/10503307.2020.1762947

Ogrodniczuk, J. S., & Piper, W. E. (1999). Measuring therapist technique in psychodynamic psychotherapies: Development and use of a new scale. *Journal of Psychotherapy Practice and Research*, *8*(2), 123–135.

Orlinsky, D. E., Rønnestad, M. H., Hartmann, A., Heinonen, E., & Willutzki, U. (2020). The personal self of psychotherapists: Dimensions, correlates, and relations with clients. *Journal of Clinical Psychology*, *76*(3), 461–475. https://doi.org/10.1002/jclp.22678

Owen, J., & Hilsenroth, M. J. (2014). Treatment adherence: The importance of therapist flexibility in relation to therapy outcomes. *Journal of Counseling Psychology*, *61*(2), 280–288. https://doi.org/10.1037/a0035753

Owen, J., Hilsenroth, M. J., & Rodolfa, E. (2013). Interaction among alliance, psychodynamic–interpersonal, and cognitive–behavioural techniques in the prediction of post-session change. *Clinical Psychology & Psychotherapy*, *19*(5), 479–489. https://doi.org/10.1002/cpp.1792

Patton, M. J., Kivlighan, D. M., Jr., & Multon, K. D. (1997). The Missouri Psychoanalytic Counseling Research Project: Relation of changes in counseling process to client outcomes. *Journal of Counseling Psychology*, *44*(2), 189–208. https://doi.org/10.1037/0022-0167.44.2.189

Power, N., Noble, L. A., Simmonds-Buckley, M., Kellett, S., Stockton, C., Firth, N., & Delgadillo, J. (2022). Associations between treatment adherence–competence–integrity and adult psychotherapy outcomes: A systematic review and meta-analysis. *Journal of Consulting and Clinical Psychology*, *90*(5), 427–445. https://doi.org/10.1037/ccp0000736

Ryum, T., Stiles, T. C., Svartberg, M., & McCullough, L. (2010). The role of transference work, the therapeutic alliance, and their interaction in reducing interpersonal problems among psychotherapy patients with Cluster C personality disorders. *Psychotherapy: Theory, Research, Practice, Training*, *47*(4), 442–453. https://doi.org/10.1037/a0021183

Sharpless, B. A. (2019). *Psychodynamic therapy techniques: A guide to expressive and supportive interventions*. Oxford University Press.

Silberschatz, G., Fretter, P. B., & Curtis, J. T. (1986). How do interpretations influence the process of psychotherapy? *Journal of Consulting and Clinical Psychology*, *54*(5), 646–652. https://doi.org/10.1037/0022-006X.54.5.646

Strachey, J. (1934). The nature of therapeutic action of psychoanalysis. *International Journal of Psychoanalysis*, *15*, 127–159.

Stricker, G., & Gold, J. R. (1996). Psychotherapy integration: An assimilative, psychodynamic approach. *Clinical Psychology: Science and Practice*, *3*(1), 47–58. https://doi.org/10.1111/j.1468-2850.1996.tb00057.x

Timulak, L., & McElvaney, R. (2013). Qualitative meta-analysis of insight events in psychotherapy. *Counselling Psychology Quarterly*, *26*(2), 131–150. https://doi.org/10.1080/09515070.2013.792997

Zilcha-Mano, S., Goldstein, P., Dolev-Amit, T., Ben David-Sela, T., & Barber, J. P. (2021). A randomized controlled trial for identifying the most suitable treatment for depression based on patients' attachment orientation. *Journal of Consulting and Clinical Psychology*, *89*(12), 985–994. https://doi.org/10.1037/ccp0000696

Part IV

Time

Evidence in Psychodynamic Psychotherapy: A Contemporary Introduction

Chapter 11

Socialization in Psychodynamic Psychotherapy

Definitions

At the initiation of therapy, the client is working to convey the problem bringing them to treatment, enter a relationship with the therapist, and decide whether psychodynamic psychotherapy (PDT) is right for them. The therapist is trying to understand the patient and their experience, create a formulation and working relationship, determine the appropriateness of PDT for the client, and produce hope and confidence for change. Researchers have identified four factors important at this stage for therapy success: socialization, selection, preferences, and expectancy. Socialization is the preparation of clients for their role in the psychotherapy process (e.g., instructions for attendance, speaking without censorship, and thinking about material between sessions) and what to expect (e.g., treatment length, symptom change, and emotional resistance). Unlike other fields of medicine in which patients are more passive and have easily discernable outcomes, psychotherapy patients are active participants in the healing and the construction of self-understanding, which may be subtle and take an indeterminate amount of time (Orne & Wender, 1968). Without explanation, the procedures of PDT could lead to genuine confusion and frustration with the therapy process. Table 11.1 gives four components to *anticipatory socialization*, a procedure early in therapy to help treatment proceed faster and avoid needless ruptures. The socialization interview is also where therapists assess the suitability of PDT for patients, or how able is the patient to be compliant with and benefit from treatment recommendations given their presentation and situation. Aptitude for PDT can be decided by a number of predictors (e.g., demographic variables, cognitive or affective abilities, psychological defenses, or type of problems) that relate to alliance, dropout, and symptom change.

DOI: 10.4324/9781003323167-16

Table 11.1 Elements for Socialization Interviews

Anticipatory Socialization (Orne & Wender, 1968)	Diagnostic Interview Assessment (Perry et al., 2008)	Suitability for Psychotherapy Scale (Laaksonen et al., 2012)
More active and directive stance	Interview frame and working ability	Affect modulation
Efforts to build rapport	Supportive interventions	Interaction flexibility
Psychoeducation about client and therapist roles	Exploration of affect	Self-observing capacity
Explanation of how therapy works	Trial defense and transference interpretations	Reflective ability
Prediction of resistance in therapy	Ability to synthesize material	Response to trial interpretation
		Problems and treatment motivation
		Target and focus

Preferences are what patients would like to have in their therapy, including activities, treatment type, and therapist characteristics (Swift et al., 2018). Preferences come from knowledge or familiarity with psychotherapy, or more recently marketing and social media use (O'Callaghan et al., 2023). Preferences can also be from individual or cultural beliefs about what causes psychological problems, attitudes about mental health and treatment, and what solutions would best resolve their problem (Bracke et al., 2019). Incorporating client preferences into the therapy increases the success of the therapy (Swift et al., 2018).

Expectancy is the hope or belief that the treatment will bring about change. Conceptually it has been divided into *credibility*, how logical or believable the treatment is, and *affective expectancy*, how much this therapy is imagined to be able to helpful (Devilly & Borkovec, 2000). Expectancy originates in attachment and transference representations, prior experiences with therapy, and individual and cultural attitudes toward mental health treatment. It can change over the course of therapy, including through therapist intervention, and is a strong predictor of outcome (Constantino et al., 2018a; 2018b).

Measurement

Trainees typically learn about socialization as part of the initial assessment and informed consent process, and templates exist in introductory psychotherapy and ethics textbooks (Gabbard, 2017). Specific interviews assess patient characteristics and aptitude for PDT. The *Dynamic Interview Adequacy* scale (Perry et al., 2008) measures how much information relevant for PDT is gained in an assessment session. Five areas evaluated are listed in Table 11.1. Separate ratings are made on each dimension for the contribution of the patient (e.g., functioning and mental capabilities), interviewer (e.g., delivery), and situation (e.g., type of problem and environment). The *Suitability for Psychotherapy Scale* (Laaksonen et al., 2012) has seven items assessing dynamic suitability (Table 11.1) based on a review of existing measures. Interestingly, these items were only weakly correlated with one another, meaning having more of one aptitude for PDT did not influence the likelihood of the patient having any other ability.

Measurement of treatment preferences is not greatly systematized (Swift et al., 2018). Participants can endorse how much they believe a list of statements about the origins of their problems ("troublesome things happened to me as a child") or the activities they think will help ("learning how to have more control over my life and my feelings") (Elkin et al., 1985). Typical categories on these are biological, interpersonal, cognitive, environmental, and spiritual. Other times participants are plainly asked which type of treatment they prefer with short descriptions of different therapy processes. The *Norcross-Cooper Preferences Inventory* (Cooper et al., 2019) is a validated measure with four dimensions that clients use to describe how they want their therapist and therapy process to be (directiveness, emotionality, past/present focus, and warmth/support). Lastly, the delay-discounting technique (Swift & Callahan, 2008), borrowed from economics and marketing research, has respondents repeatedly choose between two therapy options that are made to systematically vary on factors like symptom improvement (e.g., 50% or 80%) or research evidence (e.g., proven or experimental). Preference is the degree a participant is willing to give up one treatment option to have certain other options (e.g., giving up 30% of improvement to get a proven therapy).

Expectancy has been classically measured by the *Credibility and Expectancy Questionnaire* (Devilly & Borkovec, 2000). Patients convey their attitudes about therapy in a number of different ways ("By the end of the therapy period, how much improvement in your symptoms do you think will occur?" "At this point, how logical does the therapy offered to you seem?"). It is typically given after treatment has started so patients have knowledge to evaluate their opinions. The scaling for the questions is different (a 0–100% vs. 9-point [*not at all* to *very*] Likert scale), meaning answers have to be normed to other patients, a statistical procedure inconvenient for clinical practice. A uniquely dynamic task (Zilcha-Mano et al., 2021) was an implicit attitudes test in which the patient judged characteristics ("disappoint" and "allow") for therapists and non-therapists. The time they spent in milliseconds making their evaluation was measured, and quicker responses indicated a greater unconscious desire for the trait from their therapist. Interestingly, what patients explicitly said they wanted on an attachment measure did not always agree with what their implicit reaction suggested (Zilcha-Mano et al., 2021).

Significance

A long-established finding in psychotherapy research is when a formal socialization interview is given, patient outcome, alliance, and attendance are invariably greater (Orne & Wender, 1968). Other treatment forms are much more likely to provide socialization early in therapy but in PDT there is sometimes hesitancy to bias the therapy frame. Predictors of treatment suitability common to all therapies were also factors related to success in PDT, namely, engagement in the socialization interview, being younger, possessing verbal skills, and good premorbid functioning (Laaksonen et al., 2012; Perry et al., 2008; Valbak, 2004; Varvin, 2013). Pretreatment predictors unique to PDT are harder to isolate and paint a confusing picture in the literature. Many false positives (erroneous effects detected) and false negatives (true effects being missed) are due to small sample sizes, measurement errors, and third variables influencing therapy progress. More likely, multiple factors combine to determine a successful therapy, and in different ways for different types of persons. At present, only a handful of large-sample studies investigated multiple predictors at the same time. In these studies, patients who do especially well in PDT have less severe but more persistent depressive symptoms, more anxious distress, and more personality disorder characteristics (Cohen et al., 2019; Wienicke et al., 2023).

When treatment preferences are accommodated, patients are 75% less likely to drop out and evince a **small** effect-size toward greater improvement (Swift et al., 2018). However, research participants may differ from clients seen in practice in how they relate to their preferences. Study patients agree to accept a treatment that may not be their first choice, or even a placebo, and are assigned a therapist. Clients in real-life settings will likely have researched their provider beforehand, had initial contact before the first session, or are following a positive recommendation from a trusted other. Essentially, these clients are likely to have obtained their preferences by the time they meet their therapist and will desist at any step before beginning therapy if their wants are not satisfied. When research participants stay in a less desired therapy, even when they knowingly consented ahead of time, there is a deleterious effect on the therapy alliance over treatment (Iacoviello et al., 2007). Additionally, what clients and therapists think is preferable for treatment is rarely in line. Providers consistently want to be less directive and more emotionally involved in therapy than clients say they would prefer (Cooper et al., 2019).

Affective expectancy early in treatment has a **large** effect-size relation to eventual outcomes (Constantino et al., 2018a), even greater than that for the therapeutic alliance. Temporally, expectancy works by increasing alliance, which then is more directly associated with symptom improvement. This pathway for expectancy was proposed and tested as a mechanism of change in PDT (Joyce et al., 2003) and has since then been replicated in other types of treatments. Credibility or believability of a therapy has a **small** effect-size association with outcome in psychotherapy (Constantino et al., 2018b). Congruent with a psychodynamic and relational point-of-view, a feeling of expectation with the therapist has a more powerful impact on the therapy than an intellectual one.

New Directions

An emerging preference for clients is teletherapy. Early attempts at changing face-to-face PDT spurred concerns about breaking the therapy frame and skepticism over the validity of an online relationship. Andersson et al. (2012) developed a series of online modules to help adolescent patients identify patterns in their interpersonal relationships and then to change these maladaptive cycles with suggestions and support. Patients also messaged each week with an actual therapist about progress and questions on the modules, with nearly 80% compliance. Patients in internet-based PDT had less depression up to a year later compared to patients in a psychoeducational program. Contact with a therapist, even if it is minimal, seemed to be a critical ingredient for internet-based PDT. Mortimer and colleagues (2022) qualitatively analyzed the text of online chat sessions between therapists and adolescents in a similar internet-based PDT. Togetherness, agency, and hope emerged as underpinning a strong therapeutic alliance. Several therapist techniques contributed to these values, including displaying positivity and care, fostering a sense of collaboration, encouraging patients to take an active role, using specific praise to acknowledge progress, and preempting critical voices. Changing format is possible, but still requires a therapeutic relationship for the best effect.

PDT also can take the form of video conferencing in real time with the therapist. The worldwide COVID-19 pandemic drastically altered the practice landscape by changing technology for virtual sessions and removing legislation preventing tele-therapy. Nearly every therapist surveyed will continue meeting virtually to some degree (Aafjes-Van Doorn et al., 2024). Alliance levels and symptom outcomes in virtual therapy are equal between in-person and online treatments. However, therapists do report some changes in the process that may affect preferences, including therapist activity and disclosure, less therapist closeness and presence, and difficulty reading interpersonal cues. Patients reported similar rates (91%) of online participation in their therapy (Sousa et al., 2023). Near half of clients declared their provider never considered their preference for in-person versus virtual sessions, and 32% did not receive their desired format. Qualitative follow-up suggested that lack of choice led to less satisfaction and therapeutic alliance and more dropout (Sousa et al., 2023).

References

Aafjes-Van Doorn, K., Békés, V., Luo, X., & Hopwood, C. J. (2024). Therapists' perception of the working alliance, real relationship, and therapeutic presence in in-person therapy versus tele-therapy. *Psychotherapy Research*, *34*(5), 574–588. https://doi.org/10.1080/10503307.2023.2193299

Andersson, G., Paxling, B., Roch-Norlund, P., Östman, G., Norgren, A., Almlöv, J., & Silverberg, F. (2012). Internet-based psychodynamic versus cognitive behavioral guided self-help for generalized anxiety disorder: A randomized controlled trial. *Psychotherapy and Psychosomatics*, *81*(6), 344–355. https://doi.org/10.1159/000343073

Bracke, P., Delaruelle, K., & Verhaeghe, M. (2019). Dominant cultural and personal stigma beliefs and the utilization of mental health services: A cross-national comparison. *Frontiers in Sociology*, *4*. https://doi.org/10.3389/fsoc.2019.00040

Cohen, Z. D., Kim, T., Van, H., & Driessen, E. (2019). A demonstration of a multi-method variable selection approach for treatment selection: Recommending cognitive–behavioral versus psychodynamic therapy for mild to moderate adult depression. *Psychotherapy Research*, *30*(2), 1–14. https://doi.org/10.1080/10503307.2018.1563312

Constantino, M. J., Coyne, A. E., Boswell, J. F., Iles, B. R., & Vîslă, A. (2018a). A meta-analysis of the association between patients' early perception of treatment credibility and their posttreatment outcomes. *Psychotherapy, 55*(4), 486–495. https://doi.org/10.1037/pst0000168

Constantino, M. J., Vîslă, A., Coyne, A. E., & Boswell, J. F. (2018b). A meta-analysis of the association between patients' early treatment outcome expectation and their posttreatment outcomes. *Psychotherapy, 55*(4), 473–485. https://doi.org/10.1037/pst0000169

Cooper, M., Norcross, J. C., Raymond-Barker, B., & Hogan, T. P. (2019). Psychotherapy preferences of laypersons and mental health professionals: Whose therapy is it? *Psychotherapy, 56*(2), 205–216. https://doi.org/10.1037/pst0000226

Devilly, G. J., & Borkovec, T. D. (2000). Psychometric properties of the credibility/expectancy questionnaire. *Journal of Behavior Therapy and Experimental Psychiatry, 31*(2), 73–86. https://doi.org/10.1016/S0005-7916(00)00012-4

Elkin, I., Parloff, M. B., Hadley, S. W., & Autry, J. H. (1985). NIMH treatment of depression collaborative research program: Background and research plan. *Archives of General Psychiatry, 42*(3), 305–316. https://doi.org/10.1001/archpsyc.1985.01790260103013

Gabbard, G. O. (2017). *Long-term psychodynamic psychotherapy: A basic text* (3rd ed.). American Psychiatric Association Publishing.

Iacoviello, B. M., McCarthy, K. S., Barrett, M. S., Rynn, M., Gallop, R., & Barber, J. P. (2007). The impact of psychotherapy on patients' expectations and attitudes. *Journal of Consulting and Clinical Psychology, 75*(1), 194–198. https://doi.org/10.1037/0022-006X.75.1.194

Joyce, A. S., Ogrodniczuk, J. S., Piper, W. E., & McCallum, M. (2003). The alliance as mediator of expectancy effects in short-term individual therapy. *Journal of Consulting and Clinical Psychology, 71*(4), 672–679. https://doi.org/10.1037/0022-006X.71.4.672

Laaksonen, M. A., Lindfors, O., Knekt, P., & Aalberg, V. (2012). Suitability for psychotherapy scale and its reliability, validity, and prediction. *British Journal of Clinical Psychology, 51*(1), 1–14. https://doi.org/10.1111/j.2044-8260.2012.02033.x

Mortimer, R., Somerville, M. P., Mechler, J., Lindqvist, K., Leibovich, L., Guerrero-Tates, B., Edbrooke-Childs, J., Martin, P., & Midgley, N. (2022). Connecting over the internet: Establishing the therapeutic alliance in an internet-based treatment for depressed adolescents. *Clinical Child Psychology and Psychiatry, 27*(3), 549–568. https://doi.org/10.1177/13591045221081193

O'Callaghan, E., Belanger, H., Lucero, S., Boston, S., & Winsberg, M. (2023). Consumer expectations and attitudes about psychotherapy: Survey study. *JMIR Formative Research, 7*(1), e38696.

Orne, M. T., & Wender, P. H. (1968). Anticipatory socialization for psycho-therapy: Method and rationale. *American Journal of Psychiatry, 124*(9), 1202–1212. https://doi.org/10.1176/ajp.124.9.1202

Perry, J. C., Fowler, J. C., & Howe, A. G. (2008). Subject and interviewer determinants of the adequacy of the dynamic interview. *Journal of Nervous and Mental Disease, 196*(8), 612–619. https://doi.org/10.1097/NMD. 0b013e318181327f

Sousa, J., Smith, A., Richard, J., Rabinowitz, M., Raja, P., Mehrotra, A., Busch, A. B., Huskamp, H. A., & Uscher-Pines, L. (2023). Choosing or losing in behavioral health: A study of patients' experiences selecting telehealth versus in-person care: Study examines patient experiences selecting telehealth versus in-person care for behavioral health services. *Health Affairs, 42*(9), 1275–1282. https://doi.org/10.1377/hlthaff.2023.00487

Swift, J. K., & Callahan, J. L. (2008). A delay discounting measure of great expectations and the effectiveness of psychotherapy. *Professional Psychology: Research and Practice, 39*(6), 581–588. https://doi.org/10.1037/ 0735-7028.39.6.581

Swift, J. K., Callahan, J. L., Cooper, M., & Parkin, S. R. (2018). The impact of accommodating client preference in psychotherapy: A meta-analysis. *Journal of Clinical Psychology, 74*(11), 1924–1937. https://doi.org/10.1002/jclp.22680

Valbak, K. (2004). Suitability for psychoanalytic psychotherapy: A review. *Acta Psychiatrica Scandinavica, 109*(3), 164–178. https://doi.org/10.1046/ j.1600-0447.2003.00248.x

Varvin, S. (2013). Which patients should avoid psychoanalysis, and which professionals should avoid psychoanalytic training? A critical evaluation. *Scandinavian Psychoanalytic Review, 26*(2), 109–122. https://doi.org/10.1080/ 01062301.2003.10592919

Wienicke, F. J., Beutel, M. E., Zwerenz, R., Brähler, E., Fonagy, P., Luyten, P., Constantinou, M., Barber, J. P., McCarthy, K. S., Solomonov, N., Cooper, P. J., De Pascalis, L., Johansson, R., Andersson, G., Lemma, A., Town, J. M., Abbass, A. A., Ajilchi, B., Gibbons, M. B. C., López-Rodríguez, J., Villamil-Salcedo, V., Maina, G., Rosso, G., Twisk, J. W. R., Burk, W. J., Spijker, J., Cuijpers, P., & Driessen, E. (2023). Efficacy and moderators of short-term psychodynamic psychotherapy for depression: A systematic review and meta-analysis of individual participant data. *Clinical Psychology Review, 101*, 102269. https://doi.org/10.1016/j.cpr.2023.102269

Zilcha-Mano, S., Dolev-Amit, T., Fisher, H., Ein-Dor, T., & Strauss, B. (2021). Patients' individual differences in implicit and explicit expectations from the therapist as a function of attachment orientation. *Journal of Counseling Psychology, 68*(6), 682–695. https://doi.org/10.1037/cou0000503

Chapter 12

Working through in Psychodynamic Psychotherapy

Definitions

Working through is the middle phase of psychodynamic psychotherapy (PDT) in which the formulation is known to the patient and therapist and its ubiquity is being demonstrated. Working through involves repeatedly matching incidents in a patient's life to transference patterns until the patient is able to recognize the cycle as it happens, renounce its power, and choose to act or feel differently with some degree of autonomy. Elaboration (articulating how the transference pattern has permutated itself) and consolidation of progress (reinforcing times when insight and behavior change are applied) are the goals of this phase. Working through is less dramatic than the initial interview, "breakthrough" sessions, and termination because it involves repetition and slight, incremental changes. As a result, it received much less attention in both the clinical and the empirical literatures.

The *phase model of psychotherapy* (Howard et al., 1993) is a theory of how therapy generally unfolds that is derived from the typical "shape" seen in how clients change over time. In concept, it is the process of how humans elicit and utilize help from others. A patient loses hope, expectancy, or connection and signals this demoralization to others through anxiety, depression, or acting out. The phase model should theoretically apply to every type of helping relationship. Table 12.1 explains the timing, interventions, and changes expected for the three phases. *Remoralization* corresponds to the socialization period. Clients reconstitute from symptom distress and return to a level of prior functioning with a pledge of support from the therapist and a glimpse of a path forward. *Remediation* can be a proxy for the working through. It is the targeting of lingering symptoms and a transition to

DOI: 10.4324/9781003323167-17

Table 12.1 Phase Model of Psychotherapy

Phase	Time	Changes	Techniques
Remoralization	First several weeks	Rapid recovery in symptoms Return to function	Formation of the therapeutic relationship Increasing expectancy Specific intervention use
Remediation	Next several months	More gradual symptom improvement Consolidation of gains Beginning of well-being focus	Specific intervention use Alliance
Rehabilitation	Months to years	Growing self-enhancement Resilient functioning	Specific intervention use Real relationship

Note: Adapted from Howard et al. (1993).

an enhancement focus. Typically, short-term symptom-focused PDT terminates during or at the end of this stage (Chapter 14). Longer-term PDT or psychoanalysis will see the *rehabilitation* phase in which the patient and therapist work deeply in therapeutic relationship to make lifestyle, value, and interpersonal changes.

Measurement

When exactly working through begins and ends is different for each patient because the mid-phase of therapy is dependent on the ultimate length of the therapy. In exploratory therapy, it is not formally declared by the therapist and client. In short-term therapy, it occurs much sooner and is briefer. In psychotherapy research, *dose* is a very crude measure of the amount of therapy based on duration or number of sessions attended. Treatment dose for the typical patient has been remarkably stable over the decades, despite changes in funding structures and therapy styles (Howard et al., 1986). While a large proportion of patients will be longer term and attend many sessions, the average patient will have eight sessions (about 2 months) with their therapist. At least 50% of patients (the median) will attend at least five sessions, meaning the other half will have fewer. The most frequent course of therapy (the mode) for a patient is a single session! This fact surprises many practitioners who, looking at their own caseload, see mostly longer-term therapies. Whenever a patient commits to longer-term therapy, they take up a spot in the therapist's finite caseload, leaving diminishingly less room for new or short-term clients.

Researchers often set arbitrary timepoints for mid-phase and the assessments of process and outcome variables (e.g., Sessions 5, 10, and 15 of a 20-session therapy, Gaston et al., 1998). These scores are used singly or are aggregated to describe the treatment or predict other variables. This method assumes that the arbitrary session is important for some reason (by Session 3, the alliance is developed; Flückiger et al., 2018) or that every therapy session in that particular treatment will share the same level or score. Other investigators wait until therapy is completed and then divide sessions by the treatment length for each individual patient or partition the treatment with designations like early, middle, and late (Kivlighan et al., 2019). This method captures the elasticity of the therapy but results in different, possibly incomparable timepoints for every client.

Significance

The phase model of psychotherapy has held up to repeated testing. In therapy lasting at least four months, Stultz and Lutz (2007) found that nearly all patients improved rapidly in their well-being and symptoms within the first two months of treatment and continued to progress but more slowly for the next two months. Steady incremental changes in life functioning occurred across all four months for 80% of clients. In longer-term psychotherapies, improvements continued for months and years on symptoms and other domains like relationships, employment, and sick days, even more than for patients who received short-term therapy (Nordmo et al., 2020).

Dose-effect curves (Robinson et al., 2019) chart the average response that patients are expected to show after a particular amount of treatment compared to patients with similar pretreatment characteristics. Borrowed from the pharmaceutical literature, these statistics can identify the "minimum" number of sessions or weeks of therapy needed for a desired response, much like the prescription strength required for recovery. In this way, research can specify what an "adequate" dose of therapy is for patients to experience remission before considering a treatment to have failed. Approximately 25% of patients will improve after one session, 50% by Session 8 (2 months),

75% by Session 26 (6 months), 80% by Session 52 (1 year), and 90% by Session 104 (2 years). Dose-effect curves can "optimize" how much therapy will achieve the most outcome and avoid diminishing returns with greater treatment. These optimal amounts lie within 4–26 sessions (1–6 months; Robinson et al., 2019). However, data on which the dose-effect has been modeled rarely include longer-term patients and clients with more severe problems, and when they do, longer-term therapy provides more gain than shorter-term treatments, with 52 sessions being the optimal amount (Nordmo et al., 2020). Finally, these statistics can be used to provide feedback to therapists on whether their clients are "on-" or "off"-track compared to similar patients at that same point. Therapists can reevaluate their treatment plan for patients at risk for non-improvement, dropout, or deterioration and evidence better outcomes (Miller et al., 2015).

Empirical investigations of process changes in the working through period are much less common than studies of early therapy, largely due to research pragmatics (e.g., dropouts and missing data) than for clinical importance. In a review of the alliance–outcome literature, Flückiger et al. (2018) found 142 studies that measured alliance between Sessions 1 and 5 but only 51 during mid-treatment and 41 at termination. The correlation between alliance and outcome at termination was the strongest when measured *late* in the therapy compared to early or in mid-phase. Expressive technique in the working through period, but not other times, has been associated with subsequent outcome, seemingly in conjunction with higher alliances at the same time (Gaston et al., 1998; Kivlighan et al., 2019). Patients may be most able to engage expressive techniques in the working through than in other phases. Owen et al. (2012) found expressive techniques paired with good alliances at Session 13 prompted the patient to think about and apply more of what was discussed in therapy in between sessions.

New Directions

The success of working through could depend on clinicians' *therapeutic presence*, or their ability to remain engaged and active in the treatment. Tishby et al. (2006) found that therapeutic presence in middle phase of therapy, but not the early or later periods, differentiated good and bad therapy outcomes. Early sessions for good and bad outcome cases were similar in their levels of engagement and emotional arousal. Presence for both was increased in later sessions. In the middle of therapy, however, there was a drop in engagement, arousal, and presence in unsuccessful therapy but a continued increase for the successful case. Transference–countertransference patterns may mediate this relationship. Compared to patients who characteristically wanted recognition or felt disappointed in others, clients who wished to connect or who felt unloved had therapists who showed more engagement and more emotion as treatment progressed, ultimately relating to better alliances (Abargil & Tishby, 2021). Staying present in the mid-phase of therapy may be especially important as the dyad repeatedly works through their patterns.

References

Abargil, M., & Tishby, O. (2021). Countertransference as a reflection of the patient's inner relationship conflict. *Psychoanalytic Psychology*, *38*(1), 68–78. https://doi.org/10.1037/pap0000312

Flückiger, C., Del Re, A. C., Wampold, B. E., & Horvath, A. O. (2018). The alliance in adult psychotherapy: A meta-analytic synthesis. *Psychotherapy*, *55*(4), 316. https://doi.org/10.1037/pst0000171

Gaston, L., Thompson, L., Gallagher, D., Cournoyer, L. G., & Gagnon, R. (1998). Alliance, technique, and their interactions in predicting outcome of behavioral, cognitive, and brief dynamic therapy. *Psychotherapy Research*, *8*(2), 190–209. https://psycnet.apa.org/record/1998-04139-006

Howard, K. I., Kopta, S. M., Krause, M. S., & Orlinsky, D. E. (1986). The dose–effect relationship in psychotherapy. *American Psychologist*, *41*(2), 159–164. https://doi.org/10.1037/0003-066X.41.2.159

Howard, K. I., Lueger, R. J., Maling, M. S., & Martinovich, Z. (1993). A phase model of psychotherapy outcome: Causal mediation of change. *Journal of Consulting and Clinical Psychology*, *61*(4), 678.

Kivlighan, D. M., Hill, C. E., Ross, K., Kline, K., Furhmann, A., & Sauber, E. (2019). Testing a mediation model of psychotherapy process and outcome in psychodynamic psychotherapy: Previous client distress, psychodynamic techniques, dyadic working alliance, and current client distress. *Psychotherapy Research*, *29*(5), 581–593. https://doi.org/10.1080/10503307.2017.1420923

Miller, S. D., Hubble, M. A., Chow, D., & Seidel, J. (2015). Beyond measures and monitoring: Realizing the potential of feedback-informed treatment. *Psychotherapy*, *52*(4), 449–457.

Nordmo, M. J., Monsen, J. T., Høglend, P. A., & Solbakken, A. (2020). Investigating the dose–response effect in open-ended psychotherapy. *Psychotherapy Research*, *30*(6), 859–869. https://doi.org/10.1080/10503307.2020.1861359

Owen, J., Quirk, K., Hilsenroth, M. J., & Rodolfa, E. (2012). Working through: In-session processes that promote between-session thoughts and activities. *Journal of Counseling Psychology*, *59*(1), 161–167. https://doi.org/10.1037/a0023616

Robinson, L., Delgadillo, J., & Kellett, S. (2019). The dose-response effect in routinely delivered psychological therapies: A systematic review. *Psychotherapy Research*, *30*(1), 79–96. https://doi.org/10.1080/10503307.2019.1566676

Stultz, N., & Lutz, W. (2007). Multidimensional patterns of change in outpatient psychotherapy: The phase model revisited. *Journal of Clinical Psychology*, *63*(8), 817–833.

Tishby, O., Assa, T., & Shefler, G. (2006). Patient progress during two time-limited psychotherapies as measured by the Rutgers psychotherapy progress scale. *Psychotherapy Research*, *16*(1), 80–90. https://doi.org/10.1080/10503300500091025

Chapter 13

Termination in Psychodynamic Psychotherapy

Definitions

Termination is the formal end of therapy after which the patient and therapist agree not to have further contact (Hardy & Woodhouse, 2008). It is a specific stage of psychodynamic psychotherapy (PDT) initiated when the therapist or client recognizes a need to stop treatment. They enter into an exploration of the experience of the therapy, its ending, and the client's life without it. Termination-as-a-treatment-process is unusual among the helping professions because most provider relationships are indefinite (e.g., primary care physician) or finish without discussion after some criterion or endpoint is met (e.g., oncology specialist). Termination-as-an-intervention gives the client a chance to learn about separation from an attachment figure, prospectively and in a supportive context. Ideally, termination is *bilateral* and negotiated between patient and therapist. In open-ended therapy, the timing of termination is organic in response to needs and dynamics in the dyad. Bilateral termination does not always mean the treatment was successful. Reasons might be goal achievement, problem resolution, treatment satisfaction/dissatisfaction, reduced usefulness or overfamiliarity in the relationship, need for higher care, or alliance ruptures about separation, loss, or unmet needs. In brief PDT (see Chapter 14), the timing of the termination is agreed at the outset of treatment and is talked about throughout the therapy as opposed to just in a distinct final period.

Unilateral or *premature termination* (PT) is when one party discontinues therapy without the agreement of the other. *Dropout* or attrition is the more specific case when the patient but not the therapist wishes to terminate or when the amount of therapy received is insufficient in

DOI: 10.4324/9781003323167-18

Table 13.1 Empirically Determined Behaviors at Termination

Termination Behaviors

- Process feelings
- Focus on future
- Skill-building
- Frame development as unfinished
- Predict continued growth
- Pragmatic preparation for termination
- Reflect on gains
- Express pride and mutuality

Note: Adapted from Norcross and Zimmerman (2017).

duration or progress. In psychoanalysis, it is called an incomplete or partial analysis. PT can be for very practical reasons on the patient's side (e.g., insurance change, financial difficulties, geographical relocation, new responsibilities, physical illness, or transportation) or for more dynamic reasons (e.g., dissatisfaction with the treatment or the therapist; fear, anger, or hopelessness in the relationship). Therapists' reasons might be similar (e.g., financial reimbursement, moving location or jobs, life transitions and health issues, or expectancy the treatment will not work and would not be worth the parties' time).

Several models emphasize different experiences and processes around termination (Hardy & Woodhouse, 2008). Some models encourage insight into symptomatic reactions around loss and separation, others treat termination as an opportunity for growth, and still others emphasize therapists' ethical responsibility not to abandon clients. Norcross and Zimmerman (2017) collected 180 possible activities from treatment manuals indicated for therapists to do in the termination. Expert therapists then endorsed whether they did each. Eight factors of behaviors in the termination phase emerged, listed in Table 13.1. The type and extent of therapy determines the format of termination. More structured, active, or shorter treatments need less focus on endings while longer or open-ended treatments call for it (see Chapter 14).

Measurement

Studies on the process of bilateral termination in psychotherapy research are almost always after it has occurred (Olivera et al., 2018). When and how long termination will be is unpredictable in open-ended therapy, and the fixed timing in short-term PDT negates much of the need for negotiation. Typical retrospective methods to describe termination are exit interviews with clients and therapists, surveys about past therapy experiences, data from routine outcome monitoring programs, chart reviews, or observations of recorded final sessions. PDT adherence instruments will sometimes include items about therapists' focus on termination but rarely include a wider range of therapist behaviors that are possible as therapy ends.

Investigations of unilateral termination outnumber those on bilateral termination, and most treat PT as undesirable. They also tend to be retrospective, but some studies examine ways to prevent PT (Swift et al., 2012). Pretreatment risk factors or negative process indicators early in the treatment are used to predict dropout. One challenge is determining what signifies PT. Hatchett and Park (2003) defined PT in four ways: therapist judged PT; client did not attend a final session; client attended fewer than four sessions; and client never attended first session. They applied all four methods to every case in a large sample of clients. The different methods produced wide discrepancies in the rates of PT (41%, 41%, 53%, and 18%, respectively), and there was little agreement among definitions as to whether the same case dropped out. Therapists' judgments of PT resulted in the highest rates, alluding to a recurrent research finding that providers believe that clients should continue therapy more often than do some clients (Roos & Werbart, 2013). The operationalization of dropout has ramifications for research, as it approximates treatment acceptability (high attrition means clients did not tolerate treatment), varies among therapies for certain disorders, and determines whether an adequate dose of treatment was obtained (see Chapter 12).

Significance

Termination has often been depicted as a psychological crisis or decision point. While there are complex reactions and differences among patients, little empirical evidence exists for complicated or stormy endings in bilateral termination (Hardy & Woodhouse, 2008). Instead, over two-thirds of clients experience it as a transition or a graduation and appreciate the opportunity to talk about their therapy experience (Råbu & Haavind, 2017). Most commonly clients report a bilateral termination is due to the accomplishment of goals, and clients are twice as likely to believe their termination was for this reason than their therapists (Bartholomew et al., 2019). Positive emotions and sadness are the most frequently reported feelings by both clients and therapists at termination (Hardy & Woodhouse, 2008). Working alliance and real relationship predicted better terminations, whereas client sensitivity to loss predicted negative transference and worse outcome (Bhatia & Gelso, 2017). Therapists' own history of loss related to their likelihood of seeing sensitivity to loss in their client (Boyer & Hoffman, 1993). Treatment in psychoanalysis tends to last around 6 years (Werbart & Lagerlof, 2022). Table 13.2 lists reasons from psychoanalysts as to why treatment would be unusually long. Termination may be different for trainees than experts, as more senior therapists were more likely to have a bilateral termination than trainees (Roos & Werbart, 2013). However, nearly all trainee terminations will be premature due to the time-limited nature of many practical experiences.

PDT has typical rates of dropout compared to other forms of psychotherapy, around 20% (Swift & Greenberg, 2012). These data are mostly for brief psychotherapies. Rates may be higher in naturalistic and open-ended settings, perhaps around 35% (Roos & Werbart, 2013). Younger

Table 13.2 Psychoanalysts' Reasons for Unusually Long or Unusually Short Treatments

Unusually Long	Unusually Short
Degree or type of psychopathology • Personality disorder, trauma, and insufficient caregiving • Problem underestimated by analyst	Degree or type of psychopathology • Personality disorder, trauma, insufficient caregiving, and substance use
Analysis overly important to patients' functioning • Patient thrives in analysis and fears loss of relationship • Only supportive relationship in patient's life	Patient problems with attachment and closeness Economic or time limitations Analyst's lack of experience Negative transference or alliance rupture
Negative therapeutic reaction (losing gains) Unrealistic goals for analysis Fears that patient cannot function without	

Note: Adapted from Werbart and Lagerlof (2022).

age, male gender, less educational attainment, and greater symptom severity (especially eating disorder or trauma) predicted dropout from psychotherapy in general (Swift & Greenberg, 2012). Persons with worse psychosocial, defensive, and personality functioning at intake leave PDT at higher rates (Roos & Werbart, 2013). In military settings, individual psychotherapy had half as many dropouts as structured cognitive-behavioral therapy, especially for trauma (Penix-Smith et al., 2024. Perhaps non-directive approaches may be helpful at keeping patients in therapy than might exposure to feared stimuli. There are no good data for PT in psychoanalysis on account of its length (more time artificially creates more opportunity for dropout) and unclear definition of PT (analyses less than one year, agreement on progress and termination, and return to a psychotherapy format; Werbart & Lagerlof, 2022). Reasons psychoanalysts report for unusually short treatments are given in Table 13.2. Among training cases, dropout is around 35%, often in the first year of analysis (Glick et al., 1996).

Certain therapists experience PT at higher rates than others, accounting for 10% of the variance in why patients will drop out (Saxon et al., 2017). Interestingly, therapists with higher rates of dropout were not the same therapists whose patients worsened, suggesting patients were making judgments about continuing therapy for reasons other than symptoms. Fewer supportive interventions, negative or unempathetic therapist reactions, and infrequent or delayed contact were therapist qualities that contributed to higher dropout rates (Roos & Werbart, 2013).

New Directions

Therapists tend to believe their clients need continued therapy more often than their therapists do (Hatchett & Park, 2003; Roos & Werbart, 2013). Sometimes in these instances, we label it as a *flight into health*. The patient, frightened of the potential change that therapy can offer, suddenly experiences a relief of symptom distress and declares their wellness and frequently the need to discontinue treatment. Referenced in clinical textbooks, very little research has been done on this phenomenon. Frick (1999) reviewed case studies that followed up on patients who exhibited flight-into-health and found that, surprisingly, patients tended to remain healthy.

In psychotherapy research, sudden gains (SGs; Morrison, 2020) are when patients experience a large, significant improvement in symptoms in between two sessions. Coming from financial and actuarial fields, SGs are defined by at least a 25% drop in symptoms from one session to the next. Like Frick (1999), SGs tend to be reliable change and persist long term. About one-third of patients will experience SGs, with the average session of occurrence being the fifth session (Morrison, 2020). Having at least one SG during therapy predicts an even better outcome at termination with a **medium**-sized effect. Studies of the session preceding SGs in PDT show more accurate interpretations, better alliances, and reports from patients of problem resolution and insight (Andrusyna et al., 2006; Morrison, 2020).

References

Andrusyna, T. P., Luborsky, L., Pham, T., & Tang, T. Z. (2006). The mechanisms of sudden gains in supportive–expressive therapy for depression. *Psychotherapy Research*, *16*(5), 526–536. https://doi.org/10.1080/10503300600591379

Bartholomew, T. T., Lockard, A. J., Folger, S. F., Low, B. E., Poet, A. D., Scofield, B. E., & Locke, B. D. (2019). Symptom reduction and termination: Client change and therapist identified reasons for saying goodbye. *Counselling Psychology Quarterly*, *32*(1), 81–99. https://doi.org/10.1080/09515070.2017.1367272

Bhatia, A., & Gelso, C. J. (2017). The termination phase: Therapists' perspective on the therapeutic relationship and outcome. *Psychotherapy*, *54*(1), 76–87. https://doi.org/10.1037/pst0000100

Boyer, S. P., & Hoffman, M. A. (1993). Counselor affective reactions to termination: Impact of counselor loss history and perceived client sensitivity to loss. *Journal of Counseling Psychology*, *40*(3), 271–278. https://doi.org/10.1037/0022-0167.40.3.271

Frick, W. B. (1999). Flight into health: A new interpretation. *Journal of Humanistic Psychology*, *39*(4), 58–81. https://doi.org/10.1177/0022167899394004

Glick, R., Eagle, P., Luber, B., & Roose, S. (1996). The fate of training cases. *International Journal of Psychoanalysis*, *77*(4), 803–812.

Hardy, J. A., & Woodhouse, S. S. (2008, April). How we say goodbye: Research on psychotherapy termination. *Psychotherapy Bulletin*. https://societyforpsychotherapy.org/say-goodbye-research-psychotherapy-termination

Hatchett, G. T., & Park, H. L. (2003). Comparison of four operational definitions of premature termination. *Psychotherapy: Theory, Research, Practice, Training*, *40*(3), 226–235. https://doi.org/10.1037/0033-3204.40.3.226

Morrison, O. P. (2020). *What clients say about their single largest change in treatment: Comparing sudden gains across treatment approaches and phases of therapy* (Doctoral dissertation, University of Windsor). https://scholar.uwindsor.ca/etd/8286

Norcross, J. C., & Zimmerman, B. E. (2017). Do all therapists do that when saying goodbye? A study of commonalities in termination behaviors. *Psychotherapy*, *54*(1), 66–75. https://doi.org/10.1037/pst0000097

Olivera, J., Gomez Penedo, J. M., & Roussos, A. (2018, January). A call for "negotiation" in the termination process. *Psychotherapy Bulletin.* https://societyforpsychotherapy.org/a-call-for-negotiation-in-the-termination-process

Penix-Smith, E. A., Swift, J. K., Li, A., Bingham, J., & Hapke, G. (2024). No client left behind: A meta-analysis of premature termination from psychotherapy in U.S. service members and veterans. *American Psychologist.* Advance online publication. https://doi.org/10.1037/amp0001320

Råbu, M., & Haavind, H. (2018). Coming to terms: Client subjective experience of ending psychotherapy. *Counselling Psychology Quarterly*, *31*(2), 223–242. https://doi.org/10.1080/09515070.2017.1296410

Roos, J., & Werbart, A. (2013). Therapist and relationship factors influencing dropout from individual psychotherapy: A literature review. *Psychotherapy Research*, *23*(4), 394–418. https://doi.org/10.1080/10503307.2013.775528

Saxon, D., Firth, N., & Barkham, M. (2017). The relationship between therapist effects and therapy delivery factors: Therapy modality, dosage, and non-completion. *Administration and Policy in Mental Health and Mental Health Services Research*, *44*(6), 705–715. https://doi.org/10.1007/s10488-016-0750-5

Swift, J. K., & Greenberg, R. P. (2012). Premature discontinuation in adult psychotherapy: A meta-analysis. *Journal of Consulting and Clinical Psychology*, *80*(4), 547–559. https://doi.org/10.1037/a0028226

Swift, J. K., Greenberg, R. P., Whipple, J. L., & Kominiak, N. (2012). Practice recommendations for reducing premature termination in therapy. *Professional Psychology: Research and Practice*, *43*(4), 379–387. https://doi.org/10.1037/a0028291

Werbart, A., & Lagerlof, S. (2022). How much time does psychoanalysis take? The duration of psychoanalytic treatments from Freud's cases to the Swedish clinical practice of today. *The International Journal of Psychoanalysis*, *103*(5), 786–805. https://doi.org/10.1080/00207578.2022.2050463

Chapter 14

Time-Limited Psychodynamic Psychotherapy

Definitions

Short-term or time-limited psychodynamic therapy (PDT) is an attempt to reduce the length of treatment and optimize patient outcomes while retaining the use of dynamic principles. Evidence presented in this book is largely from studies of time-limited PDT because its format lends itself more easily to empirical investigation for reasons outlined in Table 14.1. Movement toward brief PDT originated with Ferenczi and Rank (1925), who recommended more therapist participation, heightened affect experiencing, and use of supportive interventions. However, the short duration and active therapist involvement worried psychoanalysts that time-limited PDT could trigger a *transference cure*, a temporary, unconscious

Table 14.1 Factors Supporting Development of Time-Limited Psychodynamic Psychotherapy

Empirical Advantages	Systemic Pressures
Early rapid symptom change	Competition from effective
Limited scope, easier definition, and operationalization	short-term treatments (cognitive-behavioral therapy and psychiatric
Less resources needed (money, time, and effort)	medications)
Stronger conclusions, fewer "third" variables	Rise of healthcare management organizations
Comparable length to other short-term treatments	Demands for empirical evidence of treatment efficacy
	Increased mental health awareness and need for services
	Educated consumers preferring faster, less costly symptom relief

DOI: 10.4324/9781003323167-19

improvement in symptoms to maintain the therapist's approval, instead of lasting structural personality change. Systemic factors in the 1970s caused a resurgence of brief PDTs, listed in Table 14.1. Specific models proliferated that showed the effectiveness of time-limited PDT for an array of general problems and symptoms (see Chapter 3). Treatment-resistant disorders were targeted in the next generation of short-term PDTs by extending the timeframe and incorporating perspectives from relational theory.

Short-term PDT is typically 3–4 months in length (no longer than one year), once a week for an hour, face-to-face, with a higher proportion of supportive to expressive interventions. Messer (2006) identified six commonalities of all forms of brief PDT displayed in Table 14.2. While the putative mechanisms of change (see Chapters 15–20) are thought to be the same as those in psychoanalysis, therapeutic processes in brief PDT are amplified by time-limit and therapist activity but tempered in their depth and intensity. The therapist encourages change in behavior and interpersonal relationships, linking these to the transferential patterns of the patient. The therapeutic alliance is prized both for transference work and for its direct, curative influence on the patient. Expectancy effects are fostered through goal setting

Table 14.2 Commonalities among Brief Psychodynamic Therapies

Commonalities Among Brief Psychodynamic Psychotherapies

Client selection for appropriateness	Active technique use
• Psychological mindedness and emotional maturity	• From beginning of therapy
	Agreed upon time-limit
• Ability to form a relationship and tolerate eventual separation	• Will not see each other regardless of progress or relationship
Focus on unique formulation	• Typically 3–12 months or 12–52 sessions (no longer than one year) based on complexity
• Single maladaptive interpersonal pattern	
• Brought up, connected to symptoms every session	Emphasis on termination
Goal setting	• Throughout treatment
• Symptom or problem focus	• Relation to core conflict
• Obtainable in timeframe	

Note: Adapted from Messer (2006).

and monitoring progress. Client and therapist examine transference-specific issues and solidify gains at termination but in a simpler degree than psychoanalysis because the shorter, structured relationship permits less emotional attachment and regression.

Measurement

Manualization is the set of psychoanalytic concepts and treatment guidelines that inform a treatment. Protocols for treatment in other therapies like cognitive-behavioral therapy or medication prescribing algorithms may be highly structured and limit clinicians' decision-making, often down to the activities and content for each session. As written, nearly every PDT manual is principle-based, providing possible actions for the therapist to take and theoretical and empirical rationale for their timing and use. Typically, a phasic model of therapy is proposed (evaluation, working through, and termination) proportional to the amount of time specified for the problem, a method of formulation and focus, some options and reasons for intervening, and a method to address the termination.

Significance

One of the first empirical inquiries into short-term PDT was the Menninger Psychotherapy Research Project (Wallerstein, 1989). Patients were assigned to psychoanalysis or PDT and were followed intensively over time. Psychoanalysis and PDT did equally well at changing both symptoms and psychodynamic-specific outcomes. Researchers had hypothesized better responses in psychoanalysis but drew several important conclusions from these findings. First, psychoanalysis and PDT overlapped greatly in their processes at different points in treatment. Second, alliance development was strongest with more supportive treatments, calling for a more in-depth consideration of the mechanisms and use of supportive techniques. Interpretation and expressive work continued to be important, and many patients' improvements exceeded what their therapists predicted for them at the beginning of therapy. Finally, transformations were lasting in both psychoanalysis and PDT, diminishing the likelihood of transference cure.

Many more manualized short-term PDTs have been tested for a variety of problems. In fact over 300 randomized controlled trials, experiments in which patients are assigned treatment by chance in either PDT or another comparative condition, exist for most all psychiatric presentations (Lilliengren, 2023). Outcomes evidence is reviewed in Chapter 3, but for the most common disorders and personality problems it can be said that brief PDT is certainly more effective than no treatment and is similar in effect to other treatments and medications. Patients in short- or long-term PDT or psychoanalysis do similarly well at the time of termination in the time-limited treatment (e.g., both groups assessed after 3 months) but by continuing treatment there are greater further improvements months and years after treatment initiation, with a **medium** effect-size (de Maat et al., 2013; Leichsenring et al., 2023). Importantly, studies of short-PDT show cost-effectiveness due to gains from symptom reduction and improvement in quality of life and functioning (Leichsenring et al., 2023).

Ultra-brief PDT is a model developed for patients in crisis and centered around the use of time to enhance the therapy work (de Roten et al., 2017). It is especially useful for psychiatric emergency centers, inpatient hospitals, and work with first-responder personnel. Experiencing a helping relationship during a crisis is a powerful opportunity to rework patients' expectations. Distress and visceral symptoms are likely to trigger stronger motivation to change. Often the crisis is a reenactment of interpersonal patterns, and relational learning can reach the source of the problems. Sessions are commonly massed or more frequent, allowing immediate examination of transference.

In ultra-brief PDT, therapists provide a caring, supportive relationship, formulate the interpersonal patterns precipitating the crisis, and offer trial interpretations at the end of the first session or the beginning of the next. The patient and therapist then work exclusively on the problem in the time they have, which is frequently between 3 and 12 sessions within a 1–4-week format. Termination is sudden, but the relationship, even though intense, is built with less ambivalence around the reality of ending. Ultra-brief PDTs have been shown to be effective at reducing symptoms relative to other crisis stabilization methods (de Roten et al., 2017). This area of research is notable for its thorough assessment of PDT techniques and changes in psychological defenses and transference (de Roten et al., 2017).

New Directions

One appeal of psychoanalysis and PDT over other treatments is their ability to identify and remedy unconscious conflict, the etiology of psychopathology. Surface cures cannot get at underlying problems giving rise to symptoms, and while a treatment may remove one unwanted behavior, another will simply emerge as long as the conflict remains. *Symptom substitution* is the replacement of one symptom with a new one when a cursory cure is enacted. However, this hypothesis does not seem to have evidence in the empirical literature. In both PDT and non-PDT treatments, when a person improves, for the most part they tend to stay improved months and years afterward (Leichsenring et al., 2022). This fact is shown in both primary and secondary outcomes: comorbid disorders tend to improve when the target diagnosis is improved, and new comorbidities do not emerge in the follow-up period. The exception is some medication trials, for which there may be a relapse of symptoms when the medication is withdrawn (Leichsenring et al., 2022). In describing symptom substitution, psychoanalytic theorists may not be speaking about full-blown disorder but about a repetition of the transference in a new or attenuated way. This variation in definition has not yet been tested. Alternative treatments to PDT do not often assess interpersonal patterns or motivations, and follow-up studies of PDT do not include measures of transference. While we can say comorbid symptoms do not spontaneously appear after successful but surface-level treatments, motivations and relationship patterns may still be repeating themselves in ways that influence patients' lives maladaptively.

References

de Maat, S., de Jonghe, F., de Kraker, R., Leichsenring, F., Abbass, A., Luyten, P., Barber, J. P., Van, R., & Dekker, J. (2013). The current state of the empirical evidence for psychoanalysis: A meta-analytic approach. *Harvard Review of Psychiatry*, *21*(3), 107–137. https://doi.org/10.1097/HRP.0b013e318294f5fd

de Roten, Y., Ambresin, G., Herrera, F., Ortega, D., Preisig, M., & Despland, J.-N. (2017). Efficacy of an adjunctive brief psychodynamic psychotherapy to usual inpatient treatment of depression: Results of a randomized controlled trial. *Journal of Affective Disorders*, *209*, 105–113. https://doi.org/10.1016/j.jad.2016.11.013

Ferenczi, S., & Rank, O. (1925). *The development of psycho-analysis* (C. Newton, Trans.). Nervous and Mental Disease Publishing Company.

Leichsenring, F., Abbass, A., Heim, N., Keefe, J. R., Kisely, S., Luyten, P., & Steinert, C. (2023). The status of psychodynamic psychotherapy as an empirically supported treatment for common mental disorders–An umbrella review based on updated criteria. *World Psychiatry*, *22*(2), 286–304. https://doi.org/10.1002/wps.21041

Leichsenring, F., Steinert, C., Rabung, S., & Ioannidis, J. P. A. (2022). The efficacy of psychotherapies and pharmacotherapies for mental disorders in adults: An umbrella review and meta-analytic evaluation of recent meta-analyses. *World Psychiatry*, *21*(1), 133–145. https://doi.org/10.1002/wps.20941

Lilliengren, P. (2023). A comprehensive overview of randomized controlled trials of psychodynamic psychotherapies. *Psychoanalytic Psychotherapy*, *37*(2), 117–140. https://doi.org/10.1080/02668734.2023.2197617

Messer, S. B. (2006). What makes brief psychodynamic therapy time efficient. *Clinical Psychology: Science and Practice*, *8*(1), 5–13. https://doi.org/10.1093/clipsy.8.1.5

Wallerstein, R. S. (1989). The psychotherapy research project of the Menninger Foundation: An overview. *Journal of Consulting and Clinical Psychology*, *57*(2), 195–205. https://doi.org/10.1037/0022-006X.57.2.195

Part V

Mechanisms

Evidence in Psychodynamic Psychotherapy: A Contemporary Introduction

Chapter 15

Insight in Psychodynamic Psychotherapy

Definitions

Insight is the self-understanding someone holds about their own motivations, beliefs, and behaviors. In other words, it is their awareness of their interpersonal or transferential patterns (Jennissen et al., 2018). For many, development of insight is the primary goal of psychodynamic therapy (PDT). It comes through exploration of past and present experiences and making connections across different feelings, situations, and relationships. Insight can be a sudden discovery, a "breakthrough" in resistance, or a slow iterative accumulation of knowledge in the working through. It can be both cognitive and affective in nature (McCarthy et al., 2017) although insight accompanied by feeling is more related often to symptom change. Corrective emotional experiences are when old or familiar events are experienced in a new and profound way (Alexander & French, 1946). Insight can work by making symptoms explainable, mastering a previously unsolvable situation, relieving pressure to act in problematic situations, expressing unconscious communication, or releasing emotion.

Measurement

Insight is highly individualized and carries multiple facets for a single person (e.g., the function of the symptom, the appearance of the motive, and the origin) and so eludes general properties for measurement. Most frequently, therapists have been asked to make judgments of their patients' insight, often using a single item (e.g., Mohr et al., 2015). This method, while face valid, can be influenced by therapists' countertransference, clients' problem complexity, and progress in the therapy. Open-ended questions about what factors were helpful and what changed in psychotherapy have been posed to clients, and many will answer with descriptions of insight (McCarthy et al., 2017; Timulak & McElvaney, 2013). Patients can also complete questionnaires about insight (Connolly et al., 1999; Gumz et al., 2024). The *Self-Understanding of Interpersonal Patterns* questionnaire (Connolly et al., 1999) gives patients interpersonal scenarios and asks how much each applies to themselves and their symptoms (mere recognition to a deeper understanding of historical origins). Finally, thanks to recently developed measures observers can now code patient insight from session content or interviews (Jennissen et al., 2021; Front et al., 2021; Yaffe-Herbst et al., 2023).

Significance

The experience of symptoms presumes lack of insight: being unaware should lead to problematic interactions, whereas insight should allow for satisfaction of needs. However, pretreatment levels of insight and symptoms are not related (Barber et al., 2021) and may depend on which perspective assesses insight (Front et al., 2021). Higher insight before therapy does not predict success in PDT (Barber et al., 2021; Front et al., 2021; Gumz et al., 2024) but is related to treatment retention (Mohr et al., 2015). Insight increases over the course of PDT (Barber et al., 2021; Front et al., 2021; Jennissen et al., 2021) and has a **medium**-sized effect on therapy outcomes in a meta-analysis (Jennissen et al., 2018). Symptom change with insight occurs in many different therapies but this association is stronger in PDT than in other treatments (Jennissen et al., 2018; 2021). Clients very often will report insight as an important change factor in their therapy and state that it works through poignancy in PDT but empowerment in cognitive-behavioral therapy (Timulak & McElvaney, 2013).

New Directions

Recent initiatives have brought clients to psychotherapy under the controlled influence of psychedelic medications (Reiff et al., 2020). The adaptive regression and integration of sensations from psychedelics might allow the client to experience therapy and their recollection of events in a newer, deeper, and altered way. Due to complicated ethical and legal issues, research will have challenges in conclusively showing the addition of these medications provides greater symptom relief than normal PDT or PDT with placebo. Trials of psychedelic-assisted therapy have been conducted with persons who had previous exposure to psychedelics or who were willing to try them. These volunteers are different in many ways compared to patients who would not use psychedelic medication. Their potential openness to experience and likelihood of adverse reactions might differ, as might their familiarity with psychedelic experiences (for whom placebo would be obvious). However, there does seem to be promise for the judicious use of psychedelics in PDT for certain conditions (Reiff et al., 2020). A recent poll of psychoanalysts revealed that many were cautious but open to psychedelic-assisted therapy, and expectations were higher for therapists who had taken psychedelics than for those who had not (Kraiem et al., 2024).

References

Alexander, F., & French, T. M. (1946). *Psychoanalytic therapy: Principles and application*. Ronald Press.

Barber, J. P., Muran, J. C., McCarthy, K. S., Keefe, J. R., & Zilcha-Mano, S. (2021). Research on dynamic therapies. In M. Barkham, W. Lutz, & L. G. Castonguay (Eds.), *Handbook of psychotherapy and behavior change* (6th ed., pp. 443–494). Wiley.

Connolly, M. B., Crits-Christoph, P., Shelton, R. C., Hollon, S., Kurtz, J., Barber, J. P., Butler, S. F., Baker, S., & Thase, M. E. (1999). The reliability and validity of a measure of self-understanding of interpersonal patterns. *Journal of Counseling Psychology, 46*(4), 472–482. https://doi.org/10.1037/0022-0167.46.4.472

Front, O., Yaffe-Herbst, L., Wiseman, H., Viksman, P., Kaplan, H., & Zilcha-Mano, S. (2021). Insight as a dual-perspective construct: Convergence between patients' and professional evaluators' perspective on baseline level of insight and on changes in insight. *Psychotherapy, 58*(3), 372–378. https://doi.org/10.1037/pst0000345

Gumz, A., Daubmann, A., Erices, R., Berger, J., Reuter, L., & Kästner, D. (2024). Associations between therapists' verbal techniques and patient-rated therapeutic alliance, insight, and problem solving. *Psychotherapy Research*. Advance online publication. https://doi.org/10.1080/10503307.2024.2327443

Jennissen, S., Gibbons, M. B. C., Crits-Christoph, P., Schauenburg, H., & Dinger, U. (2021). Insight as a mechanism of change in dynamic therapy for major depressive disorder. *Journal of Counseling Psychology, 68*(4), 435–445. https://doi.org/10.1037/cou0000554

Jennissen, S., Huber, J., Ehrenthal, J. C., Schauenburg, H., & Dinger, U. (2018). Association between insight and outcome of psychotherapy:

Systematic review and meta-analysis. *American Journal of Psychiatry*, *175*(10), 961–969. https://doi.org/10.1176/appi.ajp.2018.17080847

Kraiem, E., Diener, M., Guss, J., Mavrides, L., & Saban, S. (2024). Psychoanalyst attitudes towards psychedelic-assisted therapy. *Drugs: Education, Prevention and Policy*, 1–12. https://doi.org/10.1080/09687637.2024.2359444

McCarthy, K. L., Caputi, P., & Grenyer, B. F. S. (2017). Significant change events in psychodynamic psychotherapy: Is cognition or emotion more important? *Psychological Psychotherapy*, *90*(3), 377–388. https://doi.org/10.1111/papt.12116

Mohr, J. J., Fuertes, J. N., & Stracuzzi, T. I. (2015). Transference and insight in psychotherapy with gay and bisexual male clients: The role of sexual orientation identity integration. *Psychotherapy*, *52*(1), 119–126. https://doi.org/10.1037/pst0000080

Reiff, C. M., Richman, E. E., Nemeroff, C. B., Carpenter, L. L., Widge, A. S., Rodriguez, C. I., Kalin, N. H., & McDonald, W. M. (2020). Psychedelics and psychedelic-assisted psychotherapy. *American Journal of Psychiatry*, *177*(5). https://doi.org/10.1176/appi.ajp.2019.19010035

Timulak, L., & McElvaney, R. (2013). Qualitative meta-analysis of insight events in psychotherapy. *Counselling Psychology Quarterly*, *26*(2), 131–150. https://doi.org/10.1080/09515070.2013.792997

Yaffe-Herbst, L., Joffe, M., Peysachov, G., Nof, A., Gibbons, M. B. C., Crits-Christoph, P., & Zilcha-Mano, S. (2023). The development of a comprehensive coding system for evaluating insight based on a clinical interview: The SUIP-I coding system. *Psychotherapy*, *60*(2), 225–230. https://doi.org/10.1037/pst0000491

Chapter 16

Defenses in Psychodynamic Psychotherapy

Definitions

Defenses are unconscious psychological mechanisms to self-protect against anxiety over unconscious conflict or intolerable thoughts, feelings, or experiences. They manifest as inconsistencies in perceptions, logic, values, and behaviors that are seemingly not evident to the person engaging in them. Defenses work through selective attention, lapses in memory, alteration of information or experience, or unconsidered action. They are normative and universal but vary in their effectiveness to shield from anxiety, express or incorporate the intolerable, and resolve internal and external conflict. Their effectiveness corresponds to their appearance in human development, earlier being less adaptive, and hence, they are categorized by their *maturity* (Silverman & Aafjes-Van Doorn, 2023). Table 16.1 provides descriptions of defenses and their function by levels of maturity.

Many times defenses are synonymous with symptoms, like *withdrawal* in depression or *somatization* in panic. In PDT, supportive interventions reinforce defenses that promote more adaptive choices (by problem-solving the patient engages in *anticipation* or realistic planning for upcoming events; by encouraging exercise the patient *sublimates* their painful energy into goal-directed action) without addressing the unconscious conflict that sparks the anxiety. Expressive interventions break down defenses by drawing conscious awareness to their function so that they can no longer mask anxiety. In such instances, the patient comes into contact the intolerable experience and must identify new ways of managing the conflict.

DOI: 10.4324/9781003323167-22

Table 16.1 Dimensions of Psychological Defense Mechanisms

Adaptiveness	Perception	Action	Immediate	Consequences	Most Frequent Occurrence
Low	Distorting	Often	Yes	Short- and long-term	Young children Psychotic or borderline conditions
Moderate	Unchanged, or after the fact	Sometimes	Somewhat	Longer-term	Adolescents, adults Neurotic conditions
High	Enhancing or forward thinking	Rarely	No	Neither	Adults Healthier persons

Measurement

Measures of defense have been well reviewed elsewhere (Barber et al., 2021) but include interviews, projective testing, and self-report questionnaires. The *Defense Mechanism Rating Scale* (DMRS, Perry) has observers rate patients' verbal or visual expressions of 30 defenses arranged by seven maturity levels. The frequencies for individual defense use can be used but commonly the overall defensive functioning score is employed, with higher meaning more mature defenses. A recently introduced companion 30-item patient self-report (Prout et al., 2022) already has popularity in the literature. This measure produces an overall defensive functioning score and three maturity levels (mature, inhibition/avoidant, immature/depressive) that are related to other methods of assessing defense styles.

Some measures of defenses have been behaviorally or physiologically based. ISTDP measures voluntary and involuntary muscle movements or cognitive–perceptual sensations in response to therapist interventions meant to break defenses (Town et al., 2013). Social psychologists (Xu & McGregor, 2018) have creatively investigated defenses in performance-based tasks (responses to provocative stimuli or staged social encounters). Often the participant is unaware that what behaviors and perceptions are being assessed (reaction times to subliminal primes or frequency of speech errors).

Significance

Defense use is normative and only becomes problematic when the ability to see and interact with the world is impaired by ineffective or immature defenses or overemployment of certain defenses. A recent analysis of data collected by the US Census Bureau examined defense use among sample of 36,000 individuals in the community (Blanco et al., 2023). Items representing 12 defenses were pulled from a personality disorder interview ("do you rarely show much emotion?" "do you often detect hidden threats or insults in things people say or do?") and categorized by their maturity. Pathological defenses were seen in about one-third of respondents, immature defenses in three-quarters, and mature in two-thirds. Younger, never married, less educated, and lower income persons were more likely to endorse lower-maturity mature defense use. Only about 10–15% of the time did participants report the defense as impairing, but defense endorsement was more associated with self-reported mental health issues.

Research on clinical samples strongly supports lower defensive functioning is related to greater psychopathology and less improvement in psychotherapy (Barber et al., 2021; Silverman & Aafjes-Van Doorn, 2023). PDT works to broaden patients' defensive functioning level (fewer immature, more mature), and symptoms decrease when defense style also improves in therapy. Defense style can change in ultra-brief treatments, especially (see Chapter 14). Therapists use more expressive interventions when psychological defenses are less mature and alliances lower, and conversely more supportive interventions with higher defensive functioning and higher alliances (Petraglia et al., 2018), suggesting that therapists reinforce adaptive defense use and challenge maladaptive defenses. Defense style change is not unique to PDT. Most other treatments will show improvement in defensive functioning that is related to symptom change (Barber et al., 2021).

New Directions

Intensive Short-Term Dynamic Psychotherapy (ISTDP; Town et al., 2013) is a treatment in which the therapist applies gradually increasing interpersonal pressure, often multiple expressive interventions per minute, on the psychological defenses of the patient. The goal is to "unlock the unconscious" and therapists pay special attention to the psychophysiological (voluntary and involuntary muscle movements, changes in perception or in cognition) that signal defense. In accordance with theory, measurements of muscle tension and emotions changes rose then fell with clients increased insight during this session (Town et al., 2013). Patients showing this response also experienced symptom reduction, change in interpersonal behaviors, and went on to do better in a full therapy (Town et al., 2013). ISTDP is among the PDTs that has the most empirical support for somatic disorders (Abbass et al., 2020), which is consonant with its approach to psychological defense.

References

Abbass, A., Town, J., Holmes, H., Luyten, P., Cooper, A., Russell, L., Lumley, M. A., Schubiner, H., Allinson, J., Bernier, D., De Meulemeester, C., Kroenke, K., & Kisley, S. (2020). Short-term psychodynamic psychotherapy for functional somatic disorders. *Psychotherapy and Psychosomatics*, *89*(6), 363–370. https://www.jstor.org/stable/10.2307/48625575

Barber, J. P., Muran, J. C., McCarthy, K. S., Keefe, J. R., & Zilcha-Mano, S. (2021). Research on dynamic therapies. In M. Barkham, W. Lutz, & L. G. Castonguay (Eds.), *Handbook of psychotherapy and behavior change* (6th ed., pp. 443–494). Wiley.

Blanco, C., Kampe, L., Wall, M. M., Liu, S. M., Wang, S., Caligor, E., & Olfson, M. (2023). Approximating defense mechanisms in a national study of adults: Prevalence and correlates with functioning. *Translational Psychiatry*, *13*(1), 21. https://doi.org/10.1038/s41398-022-02303-3

Petraglia, J., Bhatia, M., de Roten, Y., Despland, J. N., & Drapeau, M. (2018). Investigating defense interpretation depth using lag sequential analysis. *Archives of Psychiatry and Psychotherapy*, *4*, 7–16.

Prout, T. A., Di Giuseppe, M., Zilcha-Mano, S., Perry, J. C., & Conversano, C. (2022). Psychometric properties of the Defense Mechanisms Rating Scales-Self-Report-30 (DMRS-SR-30): Internal consistency, validity, and factor structure. *Journal of Personality Assessment*, *104*(6), 833–843. https://doi.org/10.1080/00223891.2021.2019053

Silverman, J., & Aafjes-Van Doorn, K. (2023). Coping and defense mechanisms: A scoping review. *Clinical Psychology: Science and Practice*, *30*(4), 381–392. https://doi.org/10.1037/cps0000139

Town, J. M., Abbass, A., & Bernier, D. (2013). Effectiveness and cost-effectiveness of Davanloo's intensive short-term dynamic psychotherapy: Does unlocking the unconscious make a difference? *American Journal of Psychotherapy*, *67*(1), 89–103. https://doi.org/10.1176/appi.psychotherapy.2013.67.1.89

Xu, X., & McGregor, I. (2018). Motivation, threat, and defense: Perspective from experimental social psychology. *Psychological Inquiry*, *29*(1), 32–37. https://doi.org/10.1080/1047840X.2018.1435640

Chapter 17

Attachment in Psychodynamic Psychotherapy

Definitions

Attachment is perhaps the most researched concept in psychology, with over 4 million hits in a Google scholar search of the term. It is derived from object relations theory and revolves around the motive of seeking others for security and support, which later is transferred to adult relationships to promote attraction, sustained relationships, and altruistic behaviors (Levy et al., 2018). There is strong evidence for hormonal, brain, and other biological activity in the experience of attachment (Feldman, 2017), and these processes are unconscious and consonant with psychodynamic perspectives. Attachment is always in operation but becomes most noticeable in times of distress, making it highly relevant to transference patterns, how the patient perceives the therapist, and the therapeutic relationship (Levy et al., 2018).

For the psychological experience of attachment, *internal working models* of relationships are created out of actual experiences with others (Ainsworth & Bowlby, 1991). These cognitive structures store others' communications and behaviors toward the person about their worthiness of care. Later, these models process information about relationships and about the help can be expected from others in times of need. Psychodynamic therapy (PDT) examines and alters these structures, often within the therapeutic relationship. Transference from an attachment perspective is the application of these internal working models to the therapist.

Attachment styles are classifications of individuals' characteristic behaviors around eliciting, providing, and receiving help (Levy et al., 2018). Table 17.1 displays the different attachment styles and the ways they have been understood. The prevalence of these attachment styles in the population is largely stable over time but vary somewhat by cultural

DOI: 10.4324/9781003323167-23

Table 17.1 Dimensions of Attachment Styles

Categorical Style		Representations		Dimensions		Behaviors	Prevalence (%)
Children	Adults	Self	Other	Anxiety	Avoidance		
Secure	Secure	Worthy	Helpful	Low	Low	Accepts help, tolerates separation	65
Anxious-avoidant	Dismissive	Worthy	Unhelpful	Low	High	Denies help, does not value relationships	15
Anxious-ambivalent	Preoccupied	Unworthy	Helpful	High	Low	Struggles to be helped, separation intolerable	15
Disorganized	Fearful	Unworthy	Unhelpful	High	High	Not able to seek or use help	5

attitudes toward dependence. More recently, research focus has shifted to a more dimensional understanding of attachment (Fraley et al., 2011), with *attachment anxiety* (degree of relationship monitoring) and *attachment avoidance* (ability to accept help). The dimensional approach to attachment allows for a more nuanced classification of individuals, as they may not fit neatly into one attachment style for all relationships.

Measurement

Attachment has an extensive history of measurement development. Infant behavior can be observed and coded for when a caregiver leaves and returns (the *Strange Situation* task, Ainsworth & Bowlby, 1991). The comparable procedure in adults is the *Adult Attachment Interview* (AAI; George et al., 1985), a lengthy evaluation of persons' responses to questions about their relationships. Certain demand questions ask the interviewee to describe evocative experiences ("when you were upset as a child, what would you do?") or test the sophistication of their understanding of relationships ("how has your relationship with _____ changed over time?"). Both instruments produce categorizations of the attachment styles, and the AAI is also used to measure reflective functioning (Chapter 19).

Self-report instruments for adult attachment abound. The *Relationship Questionnaire* (Bartholomew & Horowitz, 1991) provides prototypes of attachment styles that participants choose among which best fits them. The *Experiences in Close Relationships Scale* (Fraley et al., 2011) measure asks survey takers to endorse the degree of certain behavioral tendencies in close relationships ("I need a lot of reassurance that I am loved by my partner") and produces scores along the attachment anxiety and avoidance dimensions. Within the therapy setting, the *Client Attachment to Therapist Scale* (Mallinckrodt et al., 1995) is specific to attachment motivations in the therapeutic setting. Items describe experiences that the client may have had ("I wish my counselor could be with me on a daily basis") and deliver three subscales on the level of secure, preoccupied, and avoidant attachment that patients show toward their therapists.

Significance

Parenting behaviors shape attachment (Fraley & Roisman, 2015), although the child's temperament and behaviors contribute strongly too. Not surprisingly, secure attachment is associated with consistent and caring behaviors sensitive to the infant's needs. Avoidant attachment is correlated with more tension, stiffness, overstimulation, and rejection in parenting. Ambivalent attachment is related to inconsistent, dependent, and emotionally labile parenting. Disorganized attachment is most associated with trauma or abuse, often at the hands of caregivers. Intergenerational transmission of attachment happens through parenting, with insecure attachments being more likely to perpetuate. Attachment generally is stable across the lifespan, but corrective experiences are possible at any age, including psychotherapy (Fraley & Roisman, 2015).

Attachment is related to emotion regulation ability and interpersonal behaviors (Eilert & Buchheim, 2023) but is *not* highly related to psychopathology (Bosman & Borelli, 2022). It is an adaptation to the early experiences of the infant and so long as the relationships in the person's life remain similar there will be good outcomes (e.g., avoidant attachment from emotional neglect will be adaptive if person continues to be surrounded by dismissive others). Adults unconsciously recreate similar environments by their willingness to get into certain types of relationships and by their response to others. New relationships prompt less attachment anxiety and avoidance when strangers match the characteristics of past relationships (see Chapter 4; Andersen & Przybylinski, 2012).

Psychotherapy is an act of helping, and client attachment influences process and outcome (Degnan et al., 2016). Anxious attachment is related to greater treatment-seeking behavior (Kealy et al., 2017), but not necessarily ability to accept help (Zilcha-Mano et al., 2021), whereas avoidance is related to less openness and disclosure in the therapy (Kealy et al., 2017). Attachment style is correlated with the strength of the alliance during therapy, with **small**, negative relations with dismissive and preoccupied attachment (Notsu et al., 2024). Much stronger correlations exist between the attachment of the patient to the therapist, with secure and dismissive, but not preoccupied, attachment to the therapist having **large** effects on alliance (Mallinkcrodt et al., 2015). Although patients with any attachment style can benefit in psychotherapy, those with a secure attachment are likely to see more improvement with a **medium**-sized effect (Levy et al., 2018). Importantly, improvement in the security of client attachment over therapy was related to better outcomes. Those with insecure attachment may do well in PDT compared to in other therapies (Levy et al., 2018; Zilcha-Mano et al., 2021).

These findings may interact with the attachment of the therapist (Degnan et al., 2016). Secure attachment on the part of the therapist can lead to stronger alliance and better outcomes among patients with higher pretreatment symptom levels, but insecure attachment was not related directly to alliance or outcome. Instead, therapist and client matching on attachment, specifically the opposite attachment styles (e.g., avoidant with ambivalent), were related to better alliances and outcomes, perhaps due to complement of the interpersonal style between the two. Preoccupied attachment in therapists increased relationship monitoring and repair, but not necessarily success at such (Marmarosh et al., 2009). Dismissing attachment styles in therapists were associated with hostile countertransference that intensified when the patient showed a preoccupied attachment (Mohr et al., 2005). These data argue for the *pathoplasticity* of attachment, meaning it is not a cause of symptomology but can be effective in a relational cure.

New Directions

Accelerated Experiential Dynamic Psychotherapy (AEDP; Fosha, 2021) is a recent attachment-centered model that integrates emotion-focused and PDT techniques to bring out the curative power of the therapeutic relationship. The attachment bond in the therapy is presupposed to occur from the first moment, but insecure attachment and emotion dysregulation prevent the patient from using it. The therapist puts focus and pressure on the therapeutic relationship to heighten it. If the patient can open to the vulnerability of being helped, the AEDP therapist can provide a secure attachment relationship in which to experience and co-regulate emotions. Distressing or defensive affects block the natural adaptive action tendencies of core affects, and therapists work to promote healthy and instructive emotions. Change is rapid, intermittent, and can occur at any moment when the patient allows for reliance on others for support and security. AEDP has shown convincing outcomes data as well as good evidence for the processes that underpin change (Iwakabe et al., 2022).

References

Ainsworth, M. D. S., & Bowlby, J. (1991). An ethological approach to personality development. *American Psychologist*, *46*(4), 331–341. https://doi.org/10.1037/0003-066X.46.4.333

Andersen, S. M., & Przybylinski, E. (2012). Experiments on transference in interpersonal relations: Implications for treatment. *Psychotherapy*, *49*(3), 370.

Bartholomew, K., & Horowitz, L. M. (1991). Attachment styles among young adults: A test of a four-category model. *Journal of Personality and Social Psychology*, *61*(2), 226–244. https://doi.org/10.1037/0022-3514.61.2.226

Bosmans, G., & Borelli, J. L. (2022). Attachment and the development of psychopathology: Introduction to the special issue. *Brain Sciences*, *12*(2), 174. https://doi.org/10.3390/brainsci12020174

Degnan, A., Seymour-Hyde, A., Harris, A., & Berry, K. (2016). The role of therapist attachment in alliance and outcome: A systematic literature review. *Clinical Psychology & Psychotherapy*, *23*(1), 47–65.

Eilert, D. W., & Buchheim, A. (2023). Attachment-related differences in emotion regulation in adults: A systematic review on attachment representations. *Brain Sciences*, *13*(6), 884. https://doi.org/10.3390/brainsci13060884

Feldman, R. (2017). The neurobiology of human attachments. *Trends in Cognitive Sciences*, *21*(2), 80–99. https://doi.org/10.1016/j.tics.2016.11.007

Fosha, D. (2021). *Undoing aloneness and the transformation of suffering into flourishing: AEDP 2.0*. American Psychological Association. https://doi.org/10.1037/0000232-015

Fraley, R. C., Heffernan, M. E., Vicary, A. M., & Brumbaugh, C. C. (2011). The experiences in close relationships—Relationship structures questionnaire: A method for assessing attachment orientations across relationships. *Psychological Assessment*, *23*(3), 615–625. https://doi.org/10.1037/a0022898

Fraley, R. C., & Roisman, G. I. (2015). Do early caregiving experiences leave an enduring or transient mark on developmental adaptation? *Current Opinion in Psychology*, *1*, 101–106. https://doi.org/10.1016/j.copsyc.2015.01.004

George, C., Kaplan, N., & Main, M. (1985). *The adult attachment interview*. Department of Psychology, University of California Berkeley.

Iwakabe, S., Edlin, J., Fosha, D., Thoma, N. C., Gretton, H., Joseph, A. J., & Nakamura, K. (2022). The long-term outcome of accelerated experiential dynamic psychotherapy: 6- and 12-month follow-up results. *Psychotherapy*, *59*(3), 431–446. https://doi.org/10.1037/pst0000441

Kealy, D., Tsai, M., & Ogrodniczuk, J. S. (2017). Attachment style and readiness for psychotherapy among psychiatric outpatients. *Psychology and Psychotherapy: Theory, Research and Practice*, *90*(2), 229–234. https://doi.org/10.1111/papt.12101

Levy, K. N., Kivity, Y., Johnson, B. N., & Gooch, C. V. (2018). Adult attachment as a predictor and moderator of psychotherapy outcome: A meta-analysis. *Journal of Clinical Psychology*, *74*(11), 1996–2013. https://doi.org/10.1002/jclp.22685

Mallinckrodt, B., Gantt, D. L., & Coble, H. M. (1995). Attachment patterns in the psychotherapy relationship: Development of the Client Attachment to Therapist Scale. *Journal of Counseling Psychology*, *42*(3), 307–317. https://doi.org/10.1037/0022-0167.42.3.307

Marmarosh, C. L., Gelso, C. J., Markin, R. D., Majors, R., Mallery, C., & Choi, J. (2009). The real relationship in psychotherapy: Relationships to adult attachments, working alliance, transference, and therapy outcome. *Journal of Counseling Psychology*, *56*(3), 337–350. https://doi.org/10.1037/a0015169

Mohr, J. J., Gelso, C. J., & Hill, C. E. (2005). Client and counselor trainee attachment as predictors of session evaluation and countertransference behavior in first counseling sessions. *Journal of Counseling Psychology*, *52*(3), 298.

Notsu, H., Blansfield, R. E., Spina, D. S., & Levy, K. N. (2024). An updated meta-analysis of the relation between adult attachment style and working alliance. *Psychotherapy Research*, 1–14. https://doi.org/10.1080/10503307.2024.2370344

Zilcha-Mano, S., Goldstein, P., Dolev-Amit, T., Ben David-Sela, T., & Barber, J. P. (2021). A randomized controlled trial for identifying the most suitable treatment for depression based on patients' attachment orientation. *Journal of Consulting and Clinical Psychology*, *89*(12), 985.

Chapter 18

Quality of Object Relations in Psychodynamic Psychotherapy

Definitions

Object relations (OR) are the cognitive and affective maps that individuals have of their interpersonal life (Barber et al., 2021; Siefert & Porcerelli, 2015), with object referring to a representation of a relationship. Developing these relationship schemas is a lifelong process involving multiple tasks, listed in Table 18.1. *Quality of object relations* (QOR) is how accurate and detailed and how useful they are to navigating relationships these representations are. QOR consists of content (valence and different persons and motivations) and structure (complexity, repetitiveness). Content depends on the early experiences of the person and the degree to which they were able to resolve specific developmental

Table 18.1 Developmental Tasks in Object Relations

Developmental Tasks in Object Relations
Populating relational map with objects in a person's life
Storing and organizing episodic and emotional information
Integrating conflicting demands and realities *within* self
Integrating conflicting demands and realities *within* relationships
• Positive and negative experiences with the same individual • Divergent motivations toward same individual
Integrating conflicting demands and realities *among* relationships
• Navigating positive experiences with persons in conflict • Reconciling hurting others achieving own motivations • Recognizing ongoing conflict in satisfying needs
Incorporating changes in relationships over time

DOI: 10.4324/9781003323167-24

challenges. Structure is how diverse and interconnected relationships are in individual's minds. Good QOR leads to perceiving interactions accurately and using past experiences to guide interpersonal behavior adaptively. Poor QOR results in recurrent or incorrect views of others, rigid ways of responding, and ultimately unsatisfying relationships.

Psychodynamic therapy (PDT) makes patients aware of their object relations, how these representations developed, and the symptoms that inflexible use of these patterns creates (Barber et al., 2021). Importantly, dynamic therapists enter into the object map as a new, healthful relationship that can be used to guide and correct other relationships. Furthermore, having greater QOR is theorized to facilitate the work of PDT. The ability to form a strong emotional bond with the therapist and to examine the misperceptions and strains that emerge in that relationship are one central pathway to change in PDT.

Measurement

As the concept of OR is broad and multidimensional, the targets and methods of measuring QOR are sundry. Determining QOR requires a more thorough assessment and a synthesis of the resulting data (Siefert & Porcerelli, 2015). In-depth relational interviews gather information about a person's social history. Frequently, respondents tell about multiple stories about relationships in their lives so that the distinctiveness of the relationships can be determined (e.g., Atzil Slonim et al., 2011; Piper et al., 2004). Projective testing has developed specific scores or composite indices that relate to QOR (Mullin et al., 2017). Self-report questionnaires rely on patients to describe their relationships and interpersonal tendencies ("I can deal with disagreements at home without disturbing family relationships," "I wish for my partner to know I am loyal") (Bell et al., 1986; Harpaz-Rotem & Blatt, 2009; Horowitz et al., 1993; McCarthy et al., 2008). One comprehensive system that measures QOR is the Operationalized Psychodynamic Diagnostic System (Zimmerman et al., 2012). It assesses the adaptiveness and maturity of basic psychological capacities, perception, regulation, communication, and attachment, for both self and for other.

How QOR is scored is equally diverse. Many instruments take the massive range of data and produce a single score or a handful of scores following a developmental maturity progression (Piper et al., 2004; Zimmerman et al., 2012). Others create a dimensional score of how much the individual endorses influence from a particular aspect or dimension of interpersonal functioning (Harpaz-Rotem & Blatt, 2009; Horowitz et al., 1993). Still others use statistical approaches that estimate rigidity or overuse of particular themes relative to the individual's interpersonal repertoire (Horowitz et al., 1993; McCarthy et al., 2008).

Significance

Research on QOR has not produced a consistent picture of its relation to symptoms, functioning, and change, probably due to how different aspects of OR contents and structure are measured across studies. When QOR includes judgments of content, especially valence in relationships, it has been related to psychological functioning and can distinguish between clinical and non-clinical samples (Barber et al., 2021). Measures of structure in QOR, however, have not produced consistent results (McCarthy et al., 2008; Zimmerman et al., 2012).

QOR may be a predictor of success in PDT but in a somewhat surprising way. Emerging evidence suggests patients with *poorer* QOR appear to do better in PDT with expressive interventions, whereas those with better QOR do well with both interpretive and supportive approaches (Aafjes-van Doorn et al., 2019; Høglend et al., 2011; Piper et al., 2004), although this effect may be dependent on the alliance. Better QOR makes it easier to form alliance, but it may be work in the relationship that is helpful to patients with lower QOR. PDT improves the content of QOR, and these changes are associated with symptom reduction over treatment (e.g., Harpaz-Rotem & Blatt, 2009; Mullin et al., 2017). Changes in structure of QOR are also consistently found in PDT but have a more complicated, perhaps curvilinear, relation to outcome (Atzil Slonim et al., 2011; McCarthy et al., 2008).

New Directions

Brain research has shed light on object relations and our experience in relationships. Mirror neurons, cells that fire when an individual both enacts a motor action and when they observe a similar action in others, have been discovered in monkeys, birds, rodents, and humans (Heyes & Catmur, 2022). These cells may facilitate learning and speech perception through observation of others, as the organism can feel, experience, or rehearse the same movements of others in their brains without having to initiate the behaviors themselves. Mirror neurons also might be important in the empathic and attachment process, helping us experience the pain or sensations of others through the mimicry firing of these neurons. However, research on these neurons is sparse and has never been conclusively linked to PDT processes.

Several interesting brain studies examined OR in the brains of depressed and never depressed persons. During a brain scan, participants hear statements that are critical, positive, or neutral that are read by the participants' mothers. Depressed patients showed more amygdalar (negative emotion) and less dorsolateral prefrontal cortex (conscious thinking) responding to negative, but not for positive and neutral, information (Hooley et al., 2009; Silk et al., 2017), suggesting that persons vulnerable to depression may have extra sensitivity to evaluations from significant others.

References

Aafjes-van Doorn, K., Kealy, D., Ehrenthal, J. C., Ogrodniczuk, J. S., Joyce, A. S., & Weber, R. (2019). Improving self-esteem through integrative group therapy for personality dysfunction: Investigating the role of the therapeutic alliance and quality of object relations. *Journal of Clinical Psychology*, 75(8), 1592–1607. https://doi.org/10.1002/jclp.22832

Atzil Slonim, D., Shefler, G., Dvir Gvirsman, S., & Tishby, O. (2011). Changes in rigidity and symptoms among adolescents in psychodynamic psychotherapy. *Psychotherapy Research*, 21(6), 685–697. https://doi.org/10.1080/10503307.2011.602753

Barber, J. P., Muran, J. C., McCarthy, K. S., Keefe, J. R., & Zilcha-Mano, S. (2021). Research on dynamic therapies. In M. Barkham, W. Lutz, & L. G. Castonguay (Eds.), *Handbook of psychotherapy and behavior change* (6th ed., pp. 443–494). Wiley.

Bell, M., Billington, R., & Becker, B. (1986). A scale for the assessment of object relations: Reliability, validity, and factorial invariance. *Journal of Clinical Psychology*, 42(5), 733–741. https://doi.org/10.1002/1097-4679(198609)42:5<733::AID-JCLP2270420509>3.0.CO;2-C

Harpaz-Rotem, I., & Blatt, S. J. (2009). A pathway to therapeutic change: Changes in self-representation in the treatment of adolescents and young adults. *Psychiatry*, 72(1), 32–48.

Heyes, C., & Catmur, C. (2022). What happened to mirror neurons? *Perspectives on Psychological Science*, 17(1), 153–168. https://doi.org/10.1177/1745691621990638

Hooley, J. M., Gruber, S. A., Parker, H. A., Guillaumot, J., Rogowska, J., & Yurgelun-Todd, D. A. (2009). Cortico-limbic response to personally challenging emotional stimuli after complete recovery from depression. *Psychiatry Research*, 172(1), 83–91. https://doi.org/10.1016/j.pscychresns.2008.12.007

Høglend, P., Hersoug, A. G., Bøgwald, K. P., Amlo, S., Marble, A., Sørbye, Ø., & Crits-Christoph, P. (2011). Effects of transference work in the context of therapeutic alliance and quality of object relations. *Journal of Consulting and Clinical Psychology*, *79*(5), 697–702. https://doi.org/10.1037/a0025115

Horowitz, L. M., Rosenberg, S. E., & Bartholomew, K. (1993). Interpersonal problems, attachment styles, and outcome in brief dynamic psychotherapy. *Journal of Consulting and Clinical Psychology*, *61*(4), 549–560. https://doi.org/10.1037/0022-006X.61.4.549

McCarthy, K. S., Gibbons, M. B. C., & Barber, J. P. (2008). The relation of rigidity across relationships with symptoms and functioning: An investigation with the revised Central Relationship Questionnaire. *Journal of Counseling Psychology*, *55*(3), 346–358. https://doi.org/10.1037/a0012578

Mullin, A. S. J., Hilsenroth, M. J., Gold, J., & Farber, B. A. (2017). Changes in object relations over the course of psychodynamic psychotherapy. *Clinical Psychology & Psychotherapy*, *24*(2), 501–511. https://doi.org/10.1002/cpp.2033

Siefert, C., & Porcerelli, J. H. (2015). Object relations theory and personality disorders: Internal representations and defense mechanisms. In S. K. Huprich (Ed.), *Personality disorders: Toward theoretical and empirical integration in diagnosis and assessment* (pp. 203–224). American Psychological Association. https://doi.org/10.1037/14549-009

Silk, J. S., Lee, K. H., Elliott, R. D., Hooley, J. M., Dahl, R. E., Barber, A., & Siegle, G. J. (2017). "Mom—I don't want to hear it": Brain response to maternal praise and criticism in adolescents with major depressive disorder. *Social Cognitive and Affective Neuroscience*, *12*(5), 729–738. https://doi.org/10.1093/scan/nsx014

Zimmermann, J., Ehrenthal, J. C., Cierpka, M., Schauenburg, H., Doering, S., & Benecke, C. (2012). Assessing the level of structural integration using operationalized psychodynamic diagnosis (OPD): Implications for DSM–5. *Journal of Personality Assessment*, *94*(5), 522–532. https://doi.org/10.1080/00223891.2012.700664

Chapter 19

Mentalization in Psychodynamic Psychotherapy

Definitions

Mentalization is the process of reflecting on ways the mental states of self and other interact with behaviors (Luyten et al., 2024). Grounded in attachment theory and theory of mind, mentalization is the comprehension of one's own and other's mental states and the use of that information to explain and guide relationship behavior. Good mentalization is a developmental achievement that occurs through empathic mirroring from early caregivers and a lack of disruptive traumatic experiences (Luyten et al., 2024). Experimentally, mentalizing emerges implicitly around 18 months when children reliably recognize their own bodies and explicitly around 4 years when they can hold in mind false beliefs and can lie to others. Understanding of intent may occur even earlier, as studies on infant morality show infants spend more time looking at helping figures and victims of harm in scenarios around 8 months (Wynn et al., 2018). Caregivers with stronger mentalization abilities tend to promote the same in their children, and trauma at this time may be related to lowered mentalization capacities (Camoirano, 2017).

Mentalization has been operationalized in research as *reflective functioning (RF)*. Those with high degrees of RF can accurately envision their own and other's cognitive and affective states, distinguish between the possible intentions in behavior, and understand how relational interactions can change and develop over time. Those with low RF capacity may struggle to take on another person's perspective or to interpret their own and others' emotional experiences, hindering engagement in secure interpersonal relationships and increasing difficulty expressing one's psychological experience. RF applies to

DOI: 10.4324/9781003323167-25

numerous conditions (borderline personality, substance dependence, eating disorders, antisocial personality), and current thinking proposes mentalization to be a transtheoretical aspect of treating any psychological concern, as all human beings utilize mentalization on a regular basis (Lutyen et al., 2024). RF has both trait- and state-like properties and can change moment-to-moment, especially in response to situational challenges (Kivity et al., 2021; Talia et al., 2019).

Measurement

The gold standard of measurement of mentalization is the *Reflective Functioning Scale* (RFS; Fonagy et al., 1998), typically coded from clinical interviews or narratives told by patients in psychotherapy. The RFS uses *demand questions* such as "do you think your childhood experiences have an influence on who you are today?" to assess RF capacities. The RFS is scored using a 9-point Likert scale that ranges from −1 (negative RF; trying not to mentalize) to 3 (ordinary RF; statements about states of mind) to 9 (exceptional RF; articulate understandings of states of mind). Additional scales to assess symptom-specific mentalization (e.g., OCD, depression, panic) have been added to the RFS. These instruments ask questions about RF around symptoms, like "Why do you think you have _____?" and "Do you associate any pattern to when you _____?" (Ekeblad et al., 2016; Kullgard et al., 2013; Rudden et al., 2006). These measures tend to be better at predicting changes in mentalization-based therapies than generic RF.

RF has also been assessed using other methods. One study examining the link between social cognition, attachment, and symptoms had participants watch the *Movie for the Assessment of Social Cognition* (Sharp et al., 2016), a tool originally used to detect autism. RF was rated from individuals' responses to videotaped social interactions. Recent validation of self-report instruments has increased the convenience of RF assessment, asking for responses that would typify response of high or lower RF like "I'm often curious about the meaning behind others' actions" (Dimitrijević et al., 2018; Fonagy et al., 2016). Some of these self-report measures have been validated for youth and across cultures. More formal adherence and competency scales (Bateman, 2020; Karterud et al., 2013; Simonsen et al., 2019) and computer coding methods (Boldrini et al., 2018) facilitate the research process at capturing this sophisticated concept.

Significance

For the most part, lower RF has been associated with greater symptoms or more severe diagnoses within studies of clinical and normative samples (Barber et al., 2021; Luyten et al., 2024). Interestingly, higher RF has been associated with better defensive functioning, specifically using more affiliation, undoing, and self-assertion and less projection, splitting, and acting out (Tanzilli et al., 2021). The amount of RF a patient enters therapy with may influence how much symptom improvement they see in PDT (Barber et al., 2021; Luyten et al., 2024). PDT promotes the increase of RF, as does emotion-focused therapy (Compare et al., 2018). Other more directive treatments may not increase RF (Barber et al., 2021; Luyten et al., 2024). Improvement in RF over treatment correlates with change in symptoms, especially when RF is tied to the understanding of symptoms (e.g., interpersonal antecedents to panic attacks).

Mentalization also has clinical implications in training. A few studies show that RF can be taught to trainees as skill, and when therapists have higher RF, their clients have better outcomes (Barber et al., 2021; Luyten et al., 2024). RF rises and decreases in a session with alliance rupture and repair as the therapist and client process the experience, especially when the therapist had a greater role in the occurrence of the rupture (Markin & McCarthy, 2024). Specific interventions like empathic reflection and interpersonal focus may increase mentalization immediately following their use (Solomonov et al., 2020; Talia et al., 2019).

New Directions

Mentalization-based treatment (MBT) is a newer PDT created for the specific purpose of improving mentalization capacities (Luyten et al., 2024). Therapeutic abstinence and neutrality (presenting the "blank slate") is not assumed by the MBT therapist, as from a two-person perspective these positions can be perceived as disengaged or disinterested. MBT entails active participation from the therapist, creating an environment where the patient can feel safe enough to explore mentalization, both strong and poor, with the clinician. The *non-mentalizing modes* (*pretend mode*, affect not matching content; *teleological mode*, disbelief of an experience not connected to concrete action; *psychic equivalence*, not separating emotion state from truth) can signal to clinicians when mentalization is compromised in the moment. The broad mechanism of change of MBT is a patient's improved capacity for interpreting the mental states of self and other and to understand the interaction of mental states. The MBT therapist often uses the therapeutic relationship as a tool to demonstrate more accurate mentalization. For example, the therapist may invite the patient to think about what the therapist could be feeling, then correct and elaborate on the accuracy of the response. MBT has demonstrated efficacy across a range of psychological problems for adults and children (Luyten et al., 2024).

References

Barber, J. P., Muran, J. C., McCarthy, K. S., Keefe, J. R., & Zilcha-Mano, S. (2021). Research on dynamic therapies. In M. Barkham, W. Lutz, & L. G. Castonguay (Eds.), *Handbook of psychotherapy and behavior change* (6th ed., pp. 443–494). Wiley.

Bateman, A. (2020). *Mentalization-based treatment adherence and competence scale*. Unpublished measure, Anna Freud Centre.

Boldrini, T., Nazzaro, M. P., Damiani, R., Genova, F., Gazzillo, F., & Lingiardi, V. (2018). Mentalization as a predictor of psychoanalytic outcome: An empirical study of transcribed psychoanalytic sessions through the lenses of a computerized text analysis measure of reflective functioning. *Psychoanalytic Psychology*, *35*(2), 196–204. https://doi.org/10.1037/pap0000136

Camoirano, A. (2017). Mentalizing makes parenting work: A review about parental reflective functioning and clinical interventions to improve it. *Frontiers in Psychology*, *8*, 14. https://doi.org/10.3389/fpsyg.2017.00014

Compare, A., Maxwell, H., Brugnera, A., Zarbo, C., Dalle Grave, R., & Tasca, G. A. (2018). Change in attachment dimensions and reflective functioning following emotionally focused group therapy for binge eating disorder. *International Journal of Group Psychotherapy*, *68*(3), 385–406. https://doi.org/10.1080/00207284.2018.1429928

Dimitrijević, A., Hanak, N., Altaras Dimitrijević, A., & Jolić Marjanović, Z. (2018). The mentalization scale (MentS): A self-report measure for the assessment of mentalizing capacity. *Journal of Personality Assessment*, *100*(3), 268–280. https://doi.org/10.1080/00223891.2017.1310730

Ekeblad, A., Falkenström, F., & Holmqvist, R. (2016). Reflective functioning as predictor of working alliance and outcome in the treatment of depression. *Journal of Consulting and Clinical Psychology*, *84*(1), 67–78. https://doi.org/10.1037/ccp0000055

Fonagy, P., Target, M., Steele, H., & Steele, M. (1998). *Reflective Functioning Scale (RF)*. Unpublished manual, University College London.

Fonagy, P., Luyten, P., Moulton-Perkins, A., Lee, Y. W., Warren, F., Howard, S., & White, C. (2016). Development and validation of a self-report measure of mentalizing: The reflective functioning questionnaire. *PLOS ONE*, *11*(7), e0158678. https://doi.org/10.1371/journal.pone.0158678

Karterud, S., Pedersen, G., Engen, M., Johansen, M. S., Johansson, P. N., Schlüter, C., & Bateman, A. W. (2013). The MBT adherence and competence scale (MBT-ACS): Development, structure and reliability. *Psychotherapy Research*, *23*(6), 705–717. https://doi.org/10.1080/10503307.2012.708795

Kivity, Y., Levy, K. N., Kelly, K. M., & Clarkin, J. F. (2021). In-session reflective functioning in psychotherapies for borderline personality disorder: The emotion regulatory role of reflective functioning. *Journal of Consulting and Clinical Psychology*, *89*(9), 751–761. https://doi.org/10.1037/ccp0000674

Kullgard, N., Persson, P., Möller, C., Falkenström, F., & Holmqvist, R. (2013). Reflective functioning in patients with obsessive–compulsive disorder (OCD)–Preliminary findings of a comparison between reflective functioning (RF) in general and OCD-specific reflective functioning. *Psychoanalytic Psychotherapy*, *27*(2), 154–169. https://doi.org/10.1080/02668734.2013.795909

Luyten, P., Campbell, C., Moser, M., & Fonagy, P. (2024). The role of mentalizing in psychological interventions in adults: Systematic review and recommendations for future research. *Clinical Psychology Review*, 102380. https://doi.org/10.1016/j.cpr.2024.102380

Markin, R. D., & McCarthy, K. S. (2024). Therapist contribution, client reflective functioning, and alliance rupture–repair: A microprocess case study of psychodynamic therapy for pregnancy after loss. *Psychotherapy*, *61*(2), 137–150. https://doi.org/10.1037/pst0000520

Rudden, M., Milrod, B., Target, M., Ackerman, S., & Graf, E. (2006). Reflective functioning in panic disorder patients: A pilot study. *Journal of the American Psychoanalytic Association*, *54*(4), 1339–1343. https://doi.org/10.1177/00030651060540040109

Sharp, C., Venta, A., Vanwoerden, S., Schramm, A., Ha, C., Newlin, E., & Fonagy, P. (2016). First empirical evaluation of the link between attachment, social cognition, and borderline features in adolescents. *Comprehensive Psychiatry*, *64*, 4–11. https://doi.org/10.1016/j.comppsych.2015.07.008

Simonsen, S., Juul, S., Kongerslev, M., Bo, S., Folmo, E., & Karterud, S. (2019). The mentalization-based therapy adherence and quality scale (MBT-AQS): Reliability in a clinical setting. *Nordic Psychology*, *71*(2), 104–115. https://doi.org/10.1080/19012276.2018.1480406

Solomonov, N., Falkenström, F., Gorman, B. S., McCarthy, K. S., Milrod, B., Rudden, M. G., Chambless, D. L., & Barber, J. P. (2020). Differential effects of alliance and techniques on Panic-Specific Reflective Function and misinterpretation of bodily sensations in two treatments for panic. *Psychotherapy Research*, *30*(1), 97–111. https://doi.org/10.1080/10503307.2019.1585591

Talia, A., Miller-Bottome, M., Katznelson, H., Pedersen, S. H., Steele, H., Schröder, P., & Taubner, S. (2019). Mentalizing in the presence of another:

Measuring reflective functioning and attachment in the therapy process. *Psychotherapy Research, 29*(5), 652–665. https://doi.org/10.1080/10503307.2017.1417651

Tanzilli, A., Di Giuseppe, M., Giovanardi, G., Boldrini, T., Caviglia, G., Conversano, C., & Lingiardi, V. (2021). Mentalization, attachment, and defense mechanisms: A Psychodynamic Diagnostic Manual-2-oriented empirical investigation. *Research in Psychotherapy: Psychopathology, Process, and Outcome, 24*(1), 531. https://doi.org/10.4081/ripppo.2021.531

Wynn, K., Bloom, P., Jordan, A., Marshall, J., & Sheskin, M. (2018). Not noble savages after all: Limits to early altruism. *Current Directions in Psychological Science, 27*(1), 3–8. https://doi.org/10.1177/0963721417734875

Chapter 20

Brain Changes in Psychodynamic Psychotherapy

Definitions

Scientific advancements in neurobiology, imaging technology, and pharmacology have produced new ways of investigating the brain and treating disorders. In prior decades, we relied on theory, happenstance accidents (neurosurgeries, traumatic brain injury), and animal models to inform our understanding. Now, brain areas and biological circuity have been charted for many integral functions like perception, memory, and self-other relatedness. Levels of specific neurotransmitters have been associated with psychological disorders, and successful treatment shows brain activity changes visible through neuroimaging (Cera et al., 2022; Fischer & Zilcha-Mano, 2022). Neuropsychoanalysis is an arising field pointing researchers toward brain anatomy and circuitry based on psychoanalytic concepts and thinking (Northoff, 2023). Exciting research for how the brain represents transference and object relations are reviewed in Chapters 4 and 18, respectively.

Terrific enthusiasm for the application of neuroscience to treatment has paralleled researchers' progress in basic science. For some, demonstrating alteration or differences in brain function is the *sine non qua* for disorder and cure. While ultimately all processes are mediated in the nervous system, much of brain research is descriptive (showing what is transpiring in the brain) and not casual (not showing why or how that came to be). If we see differences in brain activity pre- and posttreatment, we cannot say that psychodynamic therapy (PDT) made those changes or that PDT works by those differences. Many, many intermediary processes occur in between biology and behavior. Any one of them could be a mechanism for PDT. Alternatively, brain activity could be secondary or unrelated to PDT (e.g., the experience of

DOI: 10.4324/9781003323167-26

symptom recovery, and not PDT specifically, can alter what appears on a brain scan). Finally, the brain may not need to change in any appreciable way for PDT to be effective. Treatment could use the same brain circuitry as normal cognition and feeling, and states of consciousness, symbols, and meaning structures that are produced by these neural networks could be what actually changes.

Measurement

Biomarkers are molecules or other biological indicators implicated in bodily processes like stress responses, inflammation, neural activity, or environmental reactivity. Candidates typically measured in neuropsychological studies are neurotransmitters (serotonin, dopamine, norepinephrine), hormones (cortisol, oxytocin), metabolites (glutamine), and gene-expression proteins (cFOS). Changes in these indicators can be state-like (immediate) or trait-like (long-lasting). The neurotransmitter serotonin has been associated with depression in one way or another, often with the framework of genetically predisposed lower levels of serotonin contributing to greater depression. Evidence for this hypothesis is shaky (Moncrieff et al., 2023), especially due to the state-like effect that environment has on brain functioning. Artificially lowering serotonin also does not induce depression. High levels of stress also stimulate lower levels of serotonin, which may be the cause of depression.

Studies involving brain structure imaging assess which neural areas are needed for which psychological or physical operations to occur. Often the size of structures is examined, and larger structures are generally thought to mean that area is functioning more. For instance, increased white matter (networks of nerve fiber) is assumed to indicate more connectivity or signaling in the brain. Computerized tomography (CT) and magnetic resonance imaging (MRI) are two common methods in this research.

Brain activity research investigates the functional (electrical, chemical, metabolic) changes in certain neural regions or neural circuits or pathways, especially while persons perform mental or affect-provoking operations. Participants are measured at rest and then asked to do tasks while being scanned. When brain areas or circuits give more electrochemical signals or receive more blood flow, this indicates that the area is actively being called into performance. Imaging methods can show changes in the activity of the brain in real time. Functional MRI, positron emission tomography (PET), and single-photon emission computed tomography (SPECT) are common scanning methods in this research. These methods tell us the process by which specific brain areas and circuits become active during a task, like the observation of greater emotional center activity at the same time as decreased responding in self-regulation areas when depressed persons evaluated negative information (Wade-Bohleber et al., 2020). Electroencephalogram (EEG) records brainwave activity through sensors placed on the scalp and can show which brain areas are signaling or working through increased signaling. However, EEG is somewhat limited to cortical structures near the scalp, areas thought to be responsible for thinking and movement.

Significance

To conclude the brain has an important role in PDT, research must demonstrate several conditions. First, patients and healthy controls must have differing patterns of biomarkers or neural activity at baseline implicating certain brain areas in psychopathology. Then patients must show a normalization of biomarker levels or brain activity after psychotherapy to look more like healthy controls, who should not show any change over the same time period. Finally, those brain changes must be linked to symptom improvement in order for us to associate meaningfulness with those changes (i.e., patients with better outcomes show altered brain patterns while those not improving show no brain changes).

Studies involving biomarkers in psychotherapy generally reveal mixed findings. One review found interesting effects of stress (cortisol) and attachment (oxytocin) hormones in psychotherapy (Fischer & Zilcha-Mano, 2022). High levels of cortisol or low levels of oxytocin predicted worse outcomes for depression but better session outcomes for anxiety, and decreased levels or cortisol (but not oxytocin) were associated with more improvement after therapy for depression and anxiety. Oxytocin synchrony (matching levels) between client and therapist in depression was more associated pretreatment personality problems, alliance, alliance ruptures, and outcomes in PDT for depression than were mismatched levels (Fischer & Zilcha-Mano, 2022). The metabolite glutamine, synthesized after neural excitation, was increased in the anterior cingulate cortex (ACC, an area controlling emotion regulation and repetitive thinking) of depressed patients compared to healthy

Table 20.1 Brain Areas Relevant in Psychodynamic Therapy

Brain Area	Function	Location	Activity Level
Limbic system Amygdala Hypothalamus Thalamus Hippocampus	Fear and negative emotions Body regulation, physical reactions in emotion Sensory integration, sleep Memory	Midbrain, forebrain	Hyperactive
Hypothalamic–Pituitary–Adrenal Axis	Stress reaction (fight-flight response)	Midbrain, above kidneys	Elevated response, chronic
Anterior cingulate cortex	Emotion, pain and reward, repetition	Above midbrain	Hyperactive
Orbitofrontal cortex	Evaluating and making judgments	Forebrain	Hyperactive
Dorsolateral prefrontal cortex	Conscious thought, planning	Forebrain	Underactive

controls (Wade-Bohleber et al., 2023). After PDT, lower activation levels in the ACC were associated with less depression in patients, but changes in glutamine levels did not track changes in symptoms.

Functional imaging research indicates that patients and healthy persons have different levels of activity in particular brain areas related to negative emotion, decisions and planning, memory, and repetitive thought cycles (Cera et al., 2022). Table 20.1 portrays the brain regions and the direction of dysregulation implicated in many common problems like depression, anxiety, and personality difficulties. The patterns of over- and under-activation in these areas may be causal factor in the disorder or happen as a result of the disorder itself. Structural differences do not appear to be influential for differences in brain and treatment.

Normalization of brain function in these areas mentioned in Table 20.1 does appear to occur in PDT, with more upregulation in the dorsolateral prefrontal cortex (dPFC) and downregulation in orbitofrontal cortex, ACC, limbic, and hypothalamic–pituitary–adrenal (HPA) activity. This constellation of changes fits well with PDT theory of using self-reflection and reorganization of memory and experience to manage emotion reactions. Increased dPFC activation might underlie greater reflective ability and a reorganization of cognitions representing information and past experiences. The orbitofrontal cortex is a mediator between emotion, sensation, and cognitive control. Decreases in its function implies top-down regulation of emotion. Reduced ACC activity suggests corrective learning experiences and less rumination or perseveration. Finally, lowered limbic and HPA activity indicate decreased in negative emotionality and stress response, possibly due to increased emotion regulation ability or a reduced resting affective tone. Many of these changes are shared with other treatments like CBT or medication, but there may still be some pathways unique to PDT (Kalsi et al., 2017; Cera et al., 2023).

New Directions

Whereas most brain studies have been at pre–post treatment, two EEG case examples recently examined the brain during treatment itself. One combined bioneurofeedback and PDT, with every session followed by bioneurofeedback training, a method to increase concentration and enhance positive affect through brainwave monitoring). The patient showed decreases in symptoms at the same time as increases in control over positive affect, and both seemed to persist over time (Unterrainer et al., 2014). In another study (Buchheim et al., 2023), the patient was interviewed about interpersonal patterns while connected to EEG and was provided expressive interventions during the interview. EEG recordings showed decreased signaling in areas associated with sensory and motor control and increased signaling in emotional areas when there was interpretation and confrontation, suggesting that processing these experiences resulted in differing brain functioning in session similar to what behavioral studies show (see Chapter 4).

References

Buchheim, A., Kernberg, O. F., Netzer, N., Buchheim, P., Perchtold-Stefan, C., Sperner-Unterweger, B., Beckenbauer, F., & Labek, K. (2023). Differential neural response to psychoanalytic intervention techniques during structural interviewing: A single-case analysis using EEG. *Frontiers in Human Neuroscience*, *16*, 1054518. https://doi.org/10.3389/fnhum.2022.1054518

Cera, N., Monteiro, J., Esposito, R., Di Francesco, G., Cordes, D., Caldwell, J. Z. K., & Cieri, F. (2022). Neural correlates of psychodynamic and non-psychodynamic therapies in different clinical populations through fMRI: A meta-analysis and systematic review. *Frontiers in Human Neuroscience*, *16*, 1029256. https://doi.org/10.3389/fnhum.2022.1029256

Fischer, S., & Zilcha-Mano, S. (2022). Why does psychotherapy work and for whom? Hormonal answers. *Biomedicines, 10*, 1361. https://doi.org/10.3390/biomedicines10061361

Kalsi, N., Altavilla, D., Tambelli, R., Aceto, P., Trentini, C., Di Giorgio, C., & Lai, C. (2017). Neural correlates of outcome of the psychotherapy compared to antidepressant therapy in anxiety and depression disorders: A meta-analysis. *Frontiers in Psychology, 8*, 927. https://doi.org/10.3389/fpsyg.2017.00927

Moncrieff, J., Cooper, R.E., Stockmann, T., Amendola, S., Hengartner, M. P., & Horowitz, M. A. (2023). The serotonin theory of depression: A systematic umbrella review of the evidence. *Molecular Psychiatry, 28*, 3243–3256. https://doi.org/10.1038/s41380-022-01661-0

Northoff, G. (2023). *Neuropsychoanalysis: A contemporary introduction.* Routledge.

Unterrainer, H. F., Chen, M. J.-L., & Gruzelier, J. H. (2014). EEG-neurofeedback and psychodynamic psychotherapy in a case of adolescent anhedonia with substance misuse: Mood/theta relations. *International Journal of Psychophysiology, 93*(1), 84–95. https://doi.org/10.1016/j.ijpsycho.2014.03.010

Wade-Bohleber, L. M., Boeker, H., Grimm, S., Gärtner, M., Ernst, J., Recher, D. A., Bürgi, N., Seifritz, E., & Richter, A. (2020). Depression is associated with hyperconnectivity of the interoceptive socio-affective network during the recall of formative relationship episodes. *Journal of Affective Disorders, 274*, 522–534. https://doi.org/10.1016/j.jad.2020.05.110

Wade-Bohleber, L., Zoelch, N., Lehmann, M., Ernst, J., Richter, A., Seifritz, E., Boeker, H., & Grimm, S. (2023). Effects of psychotherapy on glutamatergic neurotransmission. *Neuropsychobiology, 82*(4), 203–209. https://doi.org/10.1159/000530312

Part VI

Adaptations

Evidence in Psychodynamic Psychotherapy: A Contemporary Introduction

Chapter 21

Children and Adolescents in Psychodynamic Psychotherapy

Definitions

Child psychotherapy extended psychoanalytic principles to the prevention and cure of psychological symptoms in youth and adolescents (Midgley et al., 2021). In adults, psychodynamic therapy (PDT) is largely a verbal and symbolic exercise requiring mental skills like reliable memory, self-reflection, and metacognition that may exceed children's developmental level. PDT has been adapted to meet children and adolescents' social, emotional, and cognitive capabilities and to foster understanding of their experiences that makes sense to their needs, including through the use of play. Parents can be included in the therapy process, either with their own individual sessions or with parents interacting with their child in the presence of the therapist. Importantly, child psychotherapy requires the engagement of the child in the therapy relationship, whereas cognitive-behavioral therapy for children is often skills- or contingency-based and can be performed without the direct participation of the patient (e.g., teaching parenting skills, shaping classroom environment).

Research in child and adolescent psychotherapy was slower to develop due to several reasons, such as difficulty getting the cooperation of parents or children, special ethical considerations when researching minors, and fewer clinicians and researchers that work with these populations. The most recent systematic review (Midgley et al., 2021) covered 82 studies where 22 studies were randomized control trials. Both the quality and quantity of empirical papers in this field has increased over time.

DOI: 10.4324/9781003323167-28

Measurement

Many of the research tools for adults have been adapted for children and adolescents. For instance, items on the Youth Outcome Questionnaire (Dunn et al., 2005) describe symptoms more how children might understand them ("I don't participate in activities that used to be fun," "I complain about or question rules, expectations, or responsibilities"). Versions of these same questionnaires for parents and teachers are common. In recent years, more questionnaires have been specifically developed for assessing children's psychopathology and psychotherapy outcomes. Narrative methods like interviews can be used to assess symptoms, relationships, or experiences of therapy and therapeutic gains (Loades et al., 2023).

Process observations of sessions have been taken with observer-based instruments like the Child and Adolescent Psychotherapy Process Q-Sets (Goodman, 2022). In these tools, therapist behaviors, patient behaviors, and therapist–patient interactions are ranked by the most and least representative to an individual session. In other cases, therapists take elaborate process notes for sessions with patients or parents that are later coded for themes (Creaser, 2015). Other times retrospective interviews have been used to explore the memories of adults who were in psychoanalysis as children and the meaning they gave to the experience of therapy in the context of their grownup lives (Midgley et al., 2006). Two-thirds felt that treatment had been helpful to them and only some questioned the potentially negative impact of the therapy. Many put emphasis on the importance of the experience of being listened to and understood by the therapist as the key factor for change.

Significance

The Anna Freud Centre Retrospective Study (Fonagy & Target, 1996) was perhaps the first major attempt at research and evaluation of PDT for children and adolescents. In this study, 763 closed cases of children aged between 3 and 18 years old were reviewed. Overall, 60–70% of children having moderate to severe disturbance showed reliable improvement and greater response for more intensive treatment (4–5 times weekly). Younger children benefited more than older children. A long-term follow-up study into adulthood (Schachter & Target, 2009) found that those receiving treatment in childhood were functioning well, had only a low rate of personality disorders, reported low levels of adversity, and good health with minimal use of medical services. The best predictor of adult outcome was a child's overall level of functioning before receiving treatment.

Systematic and meta-analytic reviews consistently indicate PDT's effectiveness for a wide range of mental health difficulties in children and adolescents (Midgley et al., 2021). PDT may be especially effective for internalizing disorders, emerging personality disorders, and childhood adversity compared to externalizing problems, the symptoms of which may make the development of the alliance and participation in the therapy relationship more challenging.

Child psychotherapy may work similarly to adult PDT through both supportive and expressive interventions in the therapeutic relationship. Ulberg et al. (2021) carried out an experimental study of PDT versus supportive therapy in teenagers. Adolescents in both groups improved, but depressive symptoms changed more with transference work. Halfon (2021) found the use of psychodynamic interventions was indicated in the context of a strong therapeutic alliance but may have an adverse effect if an alliance is not established. For children with comorbid or externalizing problems, keeping the relationship strong is perhaps more important (Halfon, 2021).

Youth PDT may need a higher degree of client participation and a space that allows for the expression of negative emotions. O'Keeffe and colleagues (2020) rated levels of the therapeutic alliance, any ruptures, and their resolution in recordings of therapy sessions with adolescents. Therapeutic alliance and rupture–repair during therapy were similar for therapy completers and satisfied dropouts. Premature dropouts had poorer therapeutic alliance and more unresolved ruptures. Therapists contributed to ruptures to a greater extent through minimal response, persisting with therapeutic activities, and overly focusing on risk. Similarly, Cirasola et al. (2024) identified validation, genuine interest, curiosity, and appreciation for the client as fostering a strong therapeutic alliance and facilitating rupture–repair. Negative factors were insistence on topics that the young person showed reluctance, not validating the client's thoughts and feelings explicitly, rigidly avoiding self-disclosure, lengthy, intellectualized interpretations, and ending sessions during moments of tension when time was up. These behaviors often resulted in power struggles or an increased distance between the therapist and the adolescent.

Mechanisms of change may be more experiential in child psychotherapy due to children's nascent language and cognitive abilities.

Improving mentalization or reflective functioning (RF) is a leading subject of research (see Chapter 19). Cropp et al. (2019) examined PDT in adolescents with severe symptoms and low RF scores at admission to a hospital program. Patients with RF capacities improved significantly over treatment. Changes in object relations or representations of relationships may also be an important factor of change in child psychotherapy (Atzil-Slonim et al., 2016; Bar-Kalifa & Atzil-Slomin, 2020; Blatt et al., 1996).

New Directions

PDT interventions can be helpful for parents specifically. One example is *Minding the Baby* (MTB), a program assisting young mothers at risk in terms of trauma, family instability, or complex attachment history (Slade et al., 2005). Clinicians visit mothers at home to create a relationship in which they can contemplate and then share about their own internal worlds. Mentalization techniques are used to elevate mothers' ability to hold both their babies and themselves in mind and reflect on the experiences of motherhood. Over the course of the home-visits, mothers demonstrated increased RF capacities and infants were more likely to exhibit secure attachments when compared to a control group (Slade et al., 2020). Two recent meta-analyses reviewed the PDT and parenting literature. PDT interventions improved parental RF, depression, infant behavior, and infant attachment but not parental stress or parent–infant interactions (Lo & Wong, 2022; Sleed et al., 2023). These interventions had best effect for middle childhood than for infancy or teenage years.

References

Atzil-Slonim, D., Wiseman, H., & Tishby, O. (2016). Relationship representations and change in adolescents and emerging adults during psychodynamic psychotherapy. *Psychotherapy Research*, *26*(3), 279–296. https://doi.org/10.1080/10503307.2015.1010627

Bar-Kalifa, E., & Atzil-Slonim, D. (2020). Intrapersonal and interpersonal emotional networks and their associations with treatment outcome. *Journal of Counseling Psychology*, *67*(5), 580–594. https://doi.org/10.1037/cou0000415

Blatt, S. J., Stayner, D. A., Auerbach, J. S., & Behrends, R. S. (1996). Change in object and self-representations in long-term, intensive, inpatient treatment of seriously disturbed adolescents and young adults. *Psychiatry*, *59*(1), 82–107.

Cirasola, A., Midgley, N., Muran, J. C., Eubanks, C. F., Hunter, E. B., & Fonagy, P. (2024). Repairing alliance ruptures in psychodynamic psychotherapy with young people: The development of a rational–empirical model to support youth therapists. *Psychotherapy*, *61*(1), 68–81. https://doi.org/10.1037/pst0000514

Creaser, M. (2015). *A comparison of audio recordings and therapist's process notes in child and adolescent psychoanalytic psychotherapy* (Doctoral dissertation, University of East London).

Cropp, C., Taubner, S., Salzer, S., & Streeck-Fischer, A. (2019). Psychodynamic psychotherapy with severely disturbed adolescents: Changes in reflective functioning. *Journal of Infant, Child, and Adolescent Psychotherapy*, *18*(3), 263–273. https://doi.org/10.1080/15289168.2019.1643212

Dunn, T. W., Burlingame, G. M., Walbridge, M., Smith, J., & Crum, M. J. (2005). Outcome assessment for children and adolescents: Psychometric validation of the youth outcome questionnaire 30.1 (Y-OQ®-30.1). *Clinical Psychology & Psychotherapy: An International Journal of Theory & Practice*, *12*(5), 388–401.

Fonagy, P., & Target, M. (1996). Predictors of outcome in child psychoanalysis: A retrospective study of 763 cases at the Anna Freud Centre. *Journal of the American Psychoanalytic Association*, *44*(1), 27–77.

Goodman, G. (2022). Child and adolescent psychodynamic therapy: Using Q-methodology in process research. *Psychoanalytic Study of the Child*, *75*(1), 260–277.

Halfon, S. (2021). Psychodynamic technique and therapeutic alliance in prediction of outcome in psychodynamic child psychotherapy. *Journal of Consulting and Clinical Psychology*, *89*(2), 96–109. https://doi.org/10.1037/ccp0000620

Lo, C. K., & Wong, S. Y. (2022). The effectiveness of parenting programs in regard to improving parental reflective functioning: A meta-analysis. *Attachment & Human Development*, *24*(1), 76–92.

Loades, M. E., Midgley, N., Herring, G. T., O'Keeffe, S., Goodyer, I. M., Barrett, B., & Reynolds, S. (2023). In context: Lessons about adolescent unipolar depression from the improving mood with psychoanalytic and cognitive therapies trial. *Journal of the American Academy of Child & Adolescent Psychiatry*, *63*(2), 122–135.

Midgley, N., Mortimer, R., Cirasola, A., Batra, P., & Kennedy, E. (2021). The evidence-base for psychodynamic psychotherapy with children and adolescents: A narrative synthesis. *Frontiers in Psychology*, *12*, 662671. https://doi.org/10.3389/fpsyg.2021.662671

Midgley, N., Target, M., & Smith, J. (2006). The outcome of child psychoanalysis from the patient's point of view: A qualitative analysis of a long-term follow-up study. *Psychology & Psychotherapy*, *79*(2), 257–269. https://doi.org/10.1348/147608305X52694

O'Keeffe, S., Martin, P., & Midgley, N. (2020). When adolescents stop psychological therapy: Rupture–repair in the therapeutic alliance and association with therapy ending. *Psychotherapy*, *57*(4), 471–479. https://doi.org/10.1037/pst0000287

Schachter, A., & Target, M. (2009). The adult outcome of child psychoanalysis: The Anna Freud Centre long-term follow-up study. In N. Midgley, J. Anderson, E. Grainger, T. Nesic-Vuckovic, & C. Urwin (Eds.), *Child psychotherapy and research: New approaches, emerging findings* (pp. 146–156). Routledge/Taylor & Francis Group.

Slade, A., Holland, M. L., Ordway, M. R., Carlson, E. A., Jeon, S., Close, N., Mayes, L. C., & Sadler, L. S. (2020). *Minding the Baby®*: Enhancing parental reflective functioning and infant attachment in an attachment-based, interdisciplinary home visiting program. *Development and Psychopathology*, *32*(1), 123–137.

Slade, A., Sadler, L., De Dios-Kenn, C., Webb, D., Currier-Ezepchick, J., & Mayes, L. (2005). *Minding the Baby®*: A reflective parenting program. *The Psychoanalytic Study of the Child*, *60*(1), 74–100.

Sleed, M., Li, E. T., Vainieri, I., & Midgley, N. (2023). The evidence-base for psychodynamic interventions with children under 5 years of age and their caregivers: A systematic review and meta-analysis. *Journal of Infant, Child, and Adolescent Psychotherapy*, *22*(3), 179–214.

Ulberg, R., Hummelen, B., Hersoug, A. G. Midgley, N., Høglend, P. A., & Johnsen Dahl, H.-S. (2021). The first experimental study of transference work–in teenagers (FEST–IT): A multicentre, observer- and patient-blind, randomised controlled component study. *BMC Psychiatry*, *21*, 106. https://doi.org/10.1186/s12888-021-03055-y

Chapter 22

Identity Diversity in Psychodynamic Psychotherapy

Definitions

The influence of individual and cultural diversity in psychodynamic therapy (PDT) has begun to receive the attention it deserves. Psychoanalytic principles were assumed universal and biologically based (Gundersen, 2022). Development was to tame motivations and society was an amalgamation of prohibitions and taboos, not a framework or loom for connection with others. Table 22.1 provides some traditional assumptions of PDT stemming from its Euro-American origins. Recent relational, intersubjective, feminist, and postmodern approaches opened PDT theory and practice to how therapy and the therapeutic relationship is shaped through culture (Altman, 2011; Gaztambide, 2022; Holmes et al., 2024; Love, 2022; Raque & Meisels, 2024; Tummala-Narra, 2015). Recognizing the potential of psychoanalysis, Tummala-Narra (2015) offered five theoretical ways that a relativist multicultural perspective brings PDT toward a new sense of vision, laid out in Table 22.1 in counterpoint to more traditional perspectives on PDT.

Unfortunately, research on the topic of individual and cultural diversity in PDT has lagged, not merely in topics but also the sample compositions in research (Watkins, 2012). Much important work uncovered in this review was found in unpublished dissertations (Hare, 2015; Kleiman, 2014; Mbele, 2010; Moussa, 2023; O'Toole, 2021; Okosi, 2018). Multicultural identities are as varied as human experience, and all persons have multiple intersecting identities each in their own state of development. Any review of evidence cannot account for all permutations of the identities and perspectives that are possible. To focus on wider principles for PDT and take-aways from the empirical literature, we will limit ourselves here to race/ethnicity, gender, and

DOI: 10.4324/9781003323167-29

Table 22.1 Differences Between Traditional and Multicultural Approaches to Psychodynamic Psychotherapy

Traditional Stance	Multicultural Stance
Hierarchical structure of helping relationship	Expanding self-examination
Countertransference neutrality and abstinence	
Homogeneity of experience within groups	Recognizing self-indigenous narrative
Universality of developmental experiences	Meanings of language and affect in the developmental context
Transference and session-centric attitude toward events, including experiences of racism, sexism, homo- and transphobia	Attention to social oppression
Single, unified intrapersonal identity for everyone	Multiple intersecting identities

Note: Adapted from Tummala-Narra (2015).

sexuality, knowing full well that this review is not adequate to be able to say for any person, group, or therapy dyad.

Measurement

Multicultural theories are multidisciplinary and cut across therapy orientations. The Multicultural Competencies model (Sue, 2001) has dominated the field, encompassing three therapist attributes described in Table 22.2. Therapists can build these competencies and adapt their practice to be consistent with them. In turn, having these abilities can help patients more fully develop their individual and cultural identities. The *Multicultural Counseling Inventory* (Sodowsky et al., 1994) and *Cross-Cultural Counseling Inventory* (LaFromboise et al., 1991) are questionnaires of therapists' and clients' perceptions of therapists' ability to use the three multicultural competencies.

The idea that a therapist could become "competent" suggested an endpoint in multicultural development. The *Multicultural Orientation* model (MCO; Davis et al., 2018) is a process-oriented approach that layers on PDT to facilitate exploration and connection across cultural differences. As shown in Table 22.2, MCO recognizes three processes

Table 22.2 Elements of Multicultural Competence and Multicultural Orientation Models

Multicultural Competence (Sue, 2001)		Multicultural Orientation (Owen et al., 2011)	
Awareness	Acknowledge of biases, attitudes, and systems affecting perception and behavior	Cultural humility	Openness and ability to put aside assumptions about one's own and others' cultural identity and development.
Skills	Adaptations appropriate for work with individuals from a culture	Cultural comfort	The ease into which conversations about differences are entered
Knowledge	Specific knowledge of values, practices, history and institution for a culture	Cultural opportunities	Moments in the therapy when differences in perspectives between client, therapist, and others become apparent

that operate in therapy that are cultivated through self-examination and exposure to other cultural experiences. When these experiences are present in therapy, they can be used to examine individuals' thinking and perceptions, the contexts they arose, and how each can be used to understand the situation and one another. This work is akin to transference work, promotes mentalization, and helps clients negotiate relationships more equitably and effectively. Individual scales exist measuring each of the three processes (Owen et al., 2011), and related measures exist for supervisors and groups.

Significance

Culture steers development by affording the contexts in which persons learn about themselves and the world. Others perceive and treat individuals according to their visible or known diversity factors, leading to encounters that shape interpersonal patterns in affirming, dissonant, or potentially traumatizing ways. Identity has salience for clients well before PDT begins. Getting to therapy may be a challenge for persons from populations that harbor negative attitudes and stigma toward mental health, that have experienced discrimination from providers, and that experience problems of access (Ahad et al., 2023). However, this is not the case for all populations. One group, LGBT persons, has a higher usage of therapy than their counterparts, non-LGBT persons, despite discriminatory practices historically in PDT (Burckell & Goldfried, 2006; McCarrick et al., 2020).

Clients many times have preferences about the identity factors of their therapist going into therapy. Female therapists are more requested than male therapists (Bhati, 2014) as men and women both report greater comfort disclosing to female counselors, but this literature was conducted with a binary classification of gender. Clients viewed a therapist of the same race or sexuality as beneficial, but not essential, to therapy (Burckell & Goldfried, 2006; Cabral & Smith, 2011). Swift and colleagues (2015) had participants choose between two hypothetical options for therapy: one that is highly effective therapy or one with lower effectiveness but with a therapist of a matching cultural background. Clients were willing to give up a third less symptom improvement in exchange for cultural matching. Ilagan and Heatherington (2022) replicated this study and found participants' degree of identification with a personal cultural factor accounted for cultural matching preferences.

Conversely, some clients preferred therapists of distinctly different background, especially when clients viewed their problem as external to their identity statuses (Burckell & Goldfried, 2006; Chang & Berk, 2009; Quinones et al., 2015). Ellis and colleagues (2019) presented participants with simulated therapist profiles similar to those on online directories. Therapists were portrayed as either Black or White and had or did not have a statement of commitment to serving minority populations. Black participants were more likely to prefer potential therapists by race than were White participants but statements of cultural inclusivity did not make it into their decisions. White participants were *less likely* to prefer a therapist with a diversity statement, suggesting potential reactivity around multicultural issues.

When in therapy, clients with minority identities frequently worried their therapists would not understand issues related to their life experience (Chang & Berk, 2009). They also avoided bringing up cultural concerns due to the discomfort it might cause the therapist (Chang & Berk, 2009; Dolev et al., 2018). Client–therapist similarity in race, gender, or sexuality facilitated alliance early in the therapy and has been related to clients remaining in treatment (Cabral & Smith, 2011). Identity expression was easier in part with persons of similar sexuality but therapists' helping skills were more appreciated (Quinones et al., 2015). When the therapist was perceived to have competency in working in the multicultural space, alliance and outcomes were both improved (Davis et al., 2018; Tao et al., 2015).

The therapists' own identity factors influence the experience of providing PDT, beginning with professional training. Recent psychotherapy students and analytic candidates described some stirring of attention to multicultural issues in PDT education and supervision. Most reported that instruction was color- or identity-blind, learning was insufficient to transfer to practice, or discrimination in practice and training went addressed (Moussa, 2023; O'Toole, 2021; Strong et al., 2023). Therapists just out of training were significantly more likely to report working with minority-status clients than with more seasoned clinicians (Moussa, 2023), meaning supervisors are treating different, perhaps more privileged, populations than their supervisees. To adapt, early career professionals often relied on specific relational models of multicultural orientation, self-examination and personal experiences, leaning into strong affect, and obtaining validation to help them navigate individual and cultural identity in PDT (O'Toole, 2021).

When there was an identity match between client and clinician, therapists often felt more freedom in the therapy. Therapists with a minority-status identity were more likely to express their opinions and own identity factors, use more expressive interventions, and take on more roles or functions when their clients share that identity (Goode-Cross & Grim, 2016; Mbele, 2010; Scharff et al., 2021). White therapists expressed greater discomfort and uncertainty around identity and cultural issues (Gordic, 2014; Hare, 2015; Lea et al., 2010). Almost all viewed work in the multicultural space as important but hesitated to bring it up unless the client is responsible for discussion (Hare, 2015; Kleiman, 2018). Personal experiences and self-examination were viewed as more helpful for this work then formal education (Gordic, 2014; O'Toole, 2021). Timing and careful attention to the present therapy process was also seen as critical, including gauging client's identification with the identity factor (Gordic, 2014; Lea et al., 2010). Interestingly, certain therapists achieved starkly better alliances and outcomes with clients of certain races, genders, or sexualities, although predictors of what makes these therapists effective elude us still (Hayes et al., 2016).

Therapist microaggressions toward the client are enactments in which prejudicial or transferential feelings involving race, gender, or sexuality unconsciously enter the therapy. More than half of the time, clients will experience microaggressions in their therapy, and three-quarters of the time it is never addressed (Owen et al., 2011). In an exceptional study, Okosi (2018) asked clients with a minority-status identity their experiences when their therapist committed microaggressions. Most microaggressions invalidated the client's experience of race and racism or exposed the therapist's lack of cultural knowledge. Anger was the most common reaction to microaggressions, with shock, invalidation, and disempowerment also felt. Half ended the relationship immediately, often with the client feeling it was not worth the discussion or additional burden of educating the therapist. One-third of clients explored the microaggression with their therapist, but two-thirds of these clients were the one in the dyad to initiate the conversation. When enactments around identity factors could be discussed, many clients experienced a benefit to their relationship (Kleiman, 2018; Okosi, 2018). Rupture–repair techniques were the most helpful strategies in these situations (see Chapter 7).

New Directions

Cultural acceptability of a treatment its compatibility with cultural patterns and values and its effectiveness in a certain culture, language, and context. Practice is more effective when adapted to patients' culture (Soto et al., 2018), especially when the changes are for a specific cultural group, there are many changes (compared to fewer), and the patient strongly identifies with the culture. However, few large-scale systematic modifications of PDT have been carried out and tested. White and colleagues (2006) examined guidelines in the multicultural literature and constructed a treatment manual adapting PDT for patients with an ethnic minority status. Modifications were largely to expand the use of supportive interventions, including therapist self-awareness, including questions of culture in socialization, translating goals in cultural context, acknowledging differences, expressing interest in understanding differences, and applying cultural definitions to interventions before offering. When this manual was applied, PDT was more effective than treatment as usual (Gibbons et al., 2012). Even more culturally specific adaptation is possible, and a rich theoretical and case literature gives clinicians and researchers' models for adjustment of PDT to different cultures. For example, filial piety and emotional reserve, important in many East Asian cultures, might challenge the acceptability of interpretations about the family or experiencing affect with the therapist (Duan et al., 2012; Liu, 2007). Changes in the therapeutic relationship and interventions can acculturate PDT to resonate with cultural values and expectations.

References

Ahad, A. A., Sanchez-Gonzalez, M., & Junquera, P. (2023). Understanding and addressing mental health stigma across cultures for improving psychiatric care: A narrative review. *Cureus*, *15*(5), e39549. https://doi.org/10.7759/cureus.39549

Altman, N. (2011). *The analyst in the inner city: Race, class, and culture through a psychoanalytic lens*. Routledge.

Bhati, K. S. (2014). Effect of client-therapist gender match on the therapeutic relationship: An exploratory analysis. *Psychological Reports*, *115*(2), 565–583.

Burckell, L. A., & Goldfried, M. R. (2006). Therapist qualities preferred by sexual-minority individuals. *Psychotherapy: Theory, Research, Practice, Training*, *43*(1), 32.

Cabral, R. R., & Smith, T. B. (2011). Racial/ethnic matching of clients and therapists in mental health services: A meta-analytic review of preferences, perceptions, and outcomes. *Journal of Counseling Psychology*, *58*(4), 537–554. https://doi.org/10.1037/a0025266

Chang, D. F., & Berk, A. (2009). Making cross-racial therapy work: A phenomenological study of clients' experiences of cross-racial therapy. *Journal of Counseling Psychology*, *56*(4), 521–536. https://doi.org/10.1037/a0016712

Davis, D. E., DeBlaere, C., Owen, J., Hook, J. N., Rivera, D. P., Choe, E., & Placeres, V. (2018). The multicultural orientation framework: A narrative review. *Psychotherapy*, *55*(1), 89–101. https://doi.org/10.1037/pst0000136

Dolev, T., Zilcha-Mano, S., Chui, H., Barrett, M. S., McCarthy, K. S., & Barber, J. P. (2018). The process of change in ethnic minority males undergoing psychodynamic psychotherapy: A detailed comparison of two cases. *Psychoanalytic Psychotherapy*, *32*(2), 157–180. https://doi.org/10.1080/02668734.2017.1417323

Duan, C., Hill, C., Jiang, G., Hu, B., Chui, H., Hui, K., Liu, J., & Yu, L. (2012). Therapist directives: Use and outcomes in China. *Psychotherapy Research*, *22*(4), 442–457. https://doi.org/10.1080/10503307.2012.664292

Ellis, D. M., Guastello, A. D., Anderson, P. L., & McNamara, J. P. (2019). How racially concordant therapists and culturally responsive online profiles impact treatment-seeking among Black and White Americans. *Practice Innovations*, *4*(2), 75.

Gaztambide, D. J. (2022). Love in a time of anti-Blackness: Social rank, attachment, and race in psychotherapy. *Attachment & Human Development, 24*(3), 353–365. https://doi.org/10.1080/14616734.2021.1976935

Gibbons, M. B. C., Thompson, S. M., Scott, K., Schauble, L. A., Mooney, T., Thompson, D., Green, P., MacArthur, M. J., & Crits-Christoph, P. (2012). Supportive-expressive dynamic psychotherapy in the community mental health system: A pilot effectiveness trial for the treatment of depression. *Psychotherapy, 49*(3), 303–316. https://doi.org/10.1037/a0027694

Goode-Cross, D. T., & Grim, K. A. (2016). An unspoken level of comfort": Black therapists' experiences working with black clients. *Journal of Black Psychology, 42*(1), 29–53. https://doi.org/10.1177/0095798414552103

Gordic, B. S. (2014). *Working with race and difference in cross-racial therapy dyads: An exploratory study of psychodynamic psychotherapists* (Unpublished dissertation, Rutgers University).

Gundersen, S. (2022). Mechanisms and fundamental principles in Freudian explanations. *Scandinavian Psychoanalytic Review, 45*(2), 87–95. https://doi.org/10.1080/01062301.2023.2274145

Hare, E. J. (2015). *Talking about race: How do White clinicians engage in dialogue about race cross-racial therapy with Black clients?* (Master's thesis, Smith College).

Hayes, J. A., McAleavey, A. A., Castonguay, L. G., & Locke, B. D. (2016). Psychotherapists' outcomes with White and racial/ethnic minority clients: First, the good news. *Journal of Counseling Psychology, 63*(3), 261.

Holmes, D. E., Hart, A. H., Powell, D. R., Stoute, B. J., Chodorow, N. J., Davids, M. F., Dennis, E., Glover, W., González, F. J., Hamer, F. M., Javier, R. A., Katz, M., Leary, K. R., Maree, R. D., Méndez, T., Moskowitz, M., Moss, D., Tummala-Narra, P., Ueng-McHale, J., Vaughans, K. C., Holmes, M. R., & McNamara, S. (2024). In pursuit of racial equality in American psychoanalysis: Findings and recommendations from the Holmes Commission. *Journal of the American Psychoanalytic Association, 72*(3), 407–552. https://doi.org/10.1177/00030651241253623

Ilagan, G. S., & Heatherington, L. (2022). Advancing the understanding of factors that influence client preferences for race and gender matching in psychotherapy. *Counselling Psychology Quarterly, 35*(3), 694–717. https://doi.org/10.1080/09515070.2021.1960274

Kleiman, S. (2018). *White therapists' enactments and mitigations of cultural countertransference responses in the cross-racial dyad: An interpretative phenomenological analysis* (Doctoral dissertation, University of Toronto).

LaFromboise, T. D., Coleman, H. L., & Hernandez, A. (1991). Development and factor structure of the cross-cultural counseling inventory—Revised. *Professional Psychology: Research and Practice, 22*(5), 380–388. https://doi.org/10.1037/0735-7028.22.5.380

Lea, J., Jones, R., & Huws, J. (2010). Gay psychologists and gay clients: Exploring therapist disclosure of sexuality in the therapeutic closet. *Psychology of Sexualities Review, 1*(1), 59–73.

Liu, B. (2007). *Psychotherapy with Chinese clients: the effects of cultural assumptions such as filial piety on the working relationship: A systematic literature review with illustrations from clinical practice* (Unpublished master's thesis, Auckland University of Technology).

Love, D. J. (2022). Love in a time of anti-blackness: Social rank, attachment, and race in psychotherapy. *Journal of Social and Personal Relationships*, *39*(2), 353–365. https://doi.org/10.1080/14616734.2021.1976935

Mbele, Z. (2010). *Black clinical psychologists' experiences of race in psychodynamic psychotherapy* (Doctoral dissertation, University of the Witwatersrand, Johannesburg).

McCarrick, S. M., Anderson, T., & McClintock, A. S. (2020). LGB individuals' preferences for psychotherapy theoretical orientations: Results from two studies. *Journal of Gay & Lesbian Social Services*, *32*(3), 297–309. https://doi.org/10.1080/10538720.2020.1728463

Moussa, R. (2023). Psychoanalytic and psychodynamic practitioners survey. Retrieved from https://aura.antioch.edu/etds/942

O'Toole, D. S. (2021). *Early career psychodynamic psychotherapists' experiences of incorporating culturally informed principles and approaches in clinical practice* (Doctoral dissertation, Chestnut Hill College).

Okosi, M. J. (2018). *The impact of racial microaggressions on therapeutic relationships with people of color* (Doctoral dissertation, Rutgers University).

Owen, J. J., Tao, K., Leach, M. M., & Rodolfa, E. (2011). Clients' perceptions of their psychotherapists' multicultural orientation. *Psychotherapy*, *48*(3), 274–282. https://doi.org/10.1037/a0022065

Quinones, T. J., Woodward, E. N., & Pantalone, D. W. (2015). Sexual minority reflections on their psychotherapy experiences. *Psychotherapy Research*, *25*(6), 698–708. https://doi.org/10.1080/10503307.2015.1090035

Raque, T. L., & Meisels, H. B. (2024). Structurally informed psychodynamic theory case conceptualization: Expanding the conceptualization map. *Psychotherapy*. Advance online publication. https://doi.org/10.1037/pst0000537

Scharff, A., Roberson, K., Sutherland, M. E., & Boswell, J. F. (2021). Black therapists working with Black clients: Intervention use and caseload preferences. *Practice Innovations*, *6*(2), 77–87. https://doi.org/10.1037/pri0000168

Sodowsky, G. R., Taffe, R. C., Gutkin, T. B., & Wise, S. L. (1994). Development of the Multicultural Counseling Inventory: A self-report measure of multicultural competencies. *Journal of Counseling Psychology*, *41*(2), 137–148. https://doi.org/10.1037/0022-0167.41.2.137

Soto, A., Smith, T. B., Griner, D., Domenech Rodríguez, M., & Bernal, G. (2018). Cultural adaptations and therapist multicultural competence: Two meta-analytic reviews. *Journal of Clinical Psychology*, *74*(11), 1907–1923.

Strong, Y., Flier, N., & Agrawal, H. (2023). Appealing attributes, appalling obstacles, and ideas on increasing interest in psychoanalytic training: Findings from a 2022 national survey of prospective candidates. *The American Psychoanalyst*, *57*(1), 24–29.

Sue, D. W. (2001). Multidimensional facets of cultural competence. *The Counseling Psychologist*, *29*(6), 790–821. https://doi.org/10.1177/0011000001296002

Swift, J. K., Callahan, J. L., Tompkins, K. A., Connor, D. R., & Dunn, R. (2015). A delay-discounting measure of preference for racial/ethnic matching in psychotherapy. *Psychotherapy*, *52*(3), 315.

Tao, K., Owen, J. J., Leach, M. M., & Rodolfa, E. R. (2015). A meta-analysis of multicultural competencies and psychotherapy process and outcome. *Journal of Clinical Psychology*, *74*(11), 1907–1923. https://doi.org/10.1002/jclp.22679

Tummala-Narra, P. (2015). Cultural competence as a core emphasis of psychoanalytic psychotherapy. *Psychoanalytic Psychology*, *32*(2), 275–292. https://doi.org/10.1037/a0034041

Watkins, C. E. (2012). Race/ethnicity in short-term and long-term psychodynamic psychotherapy treatment research: How "White" are the data? *Psychoanalytic Psychology*, *29*(3), 292.

White, T. M., Gibbons, M. B. C., & Schamberger, M. (2006). Cultural sensitivity and supportive expressive psychotherapy: An integrative approach to treatment. *American Journal of Psychotherapy*, *60*(3), 299–316.

Conclusion

Psychodynamic therapy (PDT) is a frequently practiced and effective treatment whose processes have been extensively validated through clinical observation, and, as the content of this book shows, through empirical methods as well. Together, the abundance of evidence for PDT should be sufficient to secure it a place in the treatment of mental disorders. We will summarize some of the highlights from empirical research on outcomes, the therapeutic relationship, interventions, and mechanisms in PDT.

PDT is an efficacious treatment. PDT improves anxiety, depression, eating, somatic, substance use, and personality symptoms in adults, adolescents, and children. It outperforms control conditions (no treatment, wait-list, or placebo) and works as well as other treatments like cognitive-behavioral therapy and psychiatric medications. Benefits from PDT remain up to two years following the end of treatment. Most empirical evidence is for brief PDTs (typically 4–26 sessions), but long-term PDT and psychoanalysis continue to show significantly greater improvement over short-term treatments. Empirical research supports that brief PDT contains many of the same processes as psychoanalysis in an attenuated form.

The therapeutic relationship is central to PDT. Patients' transference, or repetition of interpersonal patterns, links to symptoms and is altered through PDT. Initially positive transference is expressed in treatment, then negative, which is the working space for the therapist and client, and then eventually replaced by genuineness and realness for some. The strength of the therapeutic alliance is by far the strongest predictor of therapy outcome. Ruptures in the alliance can be successfully repaired with supportive interventions and here-and-now focus, often leading to improvements in outcome. Therapist feelings about

DOI: 10.4324/9781003323167-30

therapy matter. Negative countertransference predicts worse process and outcome, whereas positive countertransference must be considered in context, like the reasons for its expression.

Competent technique use, and not rigid adherence to PDT, promotes best outcome. Competence is when interventions are accurate to the formulation, are provided in a strong therapeutic alliance, and are delivered flexibly with good timing. Supportive techniques represent the majority of therapist behaviors in PDT and psychoanalysis. Both higher- and lower-functioning patients benefit from support, a fact that obscures the correlation between more supportive interventions and better outcome. Expressive interventions relate to outcome, but not simply by more provision of these techniques. Exploration and labeling of experience have a straightforward relation in which more is better. Interpretations, clarifications, and confrontations in the short-term cause disruption and discomfort in the therapy process but ultimately are associated with better outcomes, especially for persons with personality disorders.

PDT tends to follow a phase model of psychotherapy. Symptoms and functioning improve rapidly in the first few weeks and a longer period follows in which gains are slowly consolidated and a shift toward wellness and personal growth emerges. Providing anticipatory socialization (a supportive introduction to the roles and expectations for therapy) and accommodating client preferences for treatment (type, format, therapist qualities) predicts outcome and persistence in therapy. Typical client factors in therapy (higher functioning, verbal ability, expectancy for change) apply to success in PDT. Personality disorders, anxious distress, and chronic lower-grade depression may be unique predictors to PDT.

While some termination experiences can be stormy, most are associated with positive emotions, sadness over the ending, and anxiety for future functioning. About 20–35% of patients will dropout out of PDT, which is no different from other types of therapy. Risk factors for premature termination are younger age, male gender, greater symptom severity (especially eating disorder or trauma), and worse functioning.

Insight, adaptive defense mechanism use, attachment, positivity in object relations, and mentalization all increase in PDT and can be correlated with improvement in symptoms and functioning. Some are unique to PDT, but many of these mechanisms change in other forms of treatment. Inside the brain, PDT reduces activity in regions associated with negative emotionality, stress response, perseveration, and judgment and increases activity in areas for cognition and thinking. Stress and attachment hormone levels can predict better session outcomes depending on whether the patient struggles with depression or anxiety.

PDT clinicians in practice can be heartened by these results, but having an effect-size handy to quote does not meaningfully change how to treat a patient. Psychodynamic theorists can take ownership for these empirical findings and incorporate them into how we think and practice PDT. Researchers will note the familiar feeling that these findings signify a beginning, but more questions arise. We certainly need more answers for whom does PDT work best, how it creates the effects seen in these data, and how PDT practice can be augmented with empirical evidence. Essential work remains for both clinical and empirical investigators. Ending here with a quote from Freud (1930, p. 6) describes this shared endeavor: "It is hard to work with emotions scientifically."

Reference

Freud, S. (1930). *Das unbehangen in der kultur*. Internationaler Psychoanalytischer Verlag.

Index

Note: Page numbers in **bold** refer to tables.

For Product Safety Concerns and Information please contact our EU
representative GPSR@taylorandfrancis.com Taylor & Francis Verlag GmbH,
Kaufingerstraße 24, 80331 München, Germany

Printed and bound by CPI Group (UK) Ltd, Croydon, CR0 4YY
26/03/2025
01837073-0009